AMERICAN PAINTING: THE EIGHTIES

A Critical Interpretation
Barbara Rose

Photographs by Steven Sloman

in memory
Thomas B. Hess

ACKNOWLEDGMENTS

Many people have encouraged me in this project, but in particular I would like to thank Paul Haim and Jerry Leiber, and Bob and Nina Freudenheim, who shared my enthusiasm for this project. I am grateful to the artists for taking the time to write statements and to Susan Putterman for her help in all phases of putting together this book and the exhibition that inspired it. Robert Littman, Director of the Grey Art Gallery, New York, and Linda Cathcart, Director of the Contemporary Art Museum, Houston, and Judith Pisar, Chairman of the American Center, Paris, were courageous supporters of this effort. Finally, I am indebted to the Foundation Fine Art of the Century, Geneva and the SCM Corporation for their generosity.

FOREWORD

I became an art historian and a critic twenty years ago because I loved painting. When I was a student, the paintings of the New York School were widely visible at the Museum of Modern Art, and at galleries like Sidney Janis, Betty Parsons, and Sam Kootz. The artists of my generation whom I respected were those who admired Abstract Expressionism too much to imitate it. But in their wish to be original at any cost, to create an American art totally free of European conventions like drawing, illusionism, brushwork, scale, metaphor and compositional relationships, they finally arrived at styles that I ultimately found lacking the qualities that had drawn me to the study of art in the first place.

And so, with very few exceptions, I stopped writing about contemporary art. Nothing in object art, conceptual art, performance, video or even photography and film, which could have a claim to more than narcissistic exhibitionism, moved me as painting had. I shared the disgust of painters who rejected abstract art in favor of realism for the cynicism, nihilism, demoralization and contempt toward both the public and their craft that so called artists, lacking faith in the future, displayed in ephemeral art and works made of materials destined to disintegrate. Yet I could not believe in a retardataire "return to realism" that jettisoned those fundamentals of modernism that artists since Cézanne had fought to establish. In good conscience, I could not pretend that the last seventy years of the evolution of a self-awareness and an awareness of the properties of art and art making never happened.

Thus I found myself isolated, revolted by the excesses and extremes to which the idea of art as tradition-smashing revolution had been taken, but unable to identify with the other extreme of a wholesale conversion to the exhausted conventions of the art of the last century. Once I had looked for community to an art world that had disintegrated into a petty, squabbling armed camp of internecine quarrels, power mongering, self-promotion, mate-rialism and egos inflated by premature adulation. In the galleries I saw eccentric sensational ploys to gain attention. SoHo made me nostalgic for Tenth Street, where the art was bad enough, but at least it was art and not some social, political or promotional statement made in its name. I returned to the study of the Old Masters, the modern masters, and earlier American modernists who had not felt it necessary to reject all that had gone before them to make important new art. Although I continued to visit galleries and modern art museums, it was obvious that the dealers were playing follow the leader, and the curators were for their part following the lead of the dealers. Since those of my colleagues whom I had once learned from had ceased writing for the art magazines, with little regret, I gave up reading them as well.

Sometimes in the Metropolitan or the Frick, I would run into a young artist. We would talk about El Greco or Velazquez of Ingres, or about Leo Steinberg's Other Criteria, his essays emphasizing the similarities between the Old Masters and the modern masters, as opposed to their differences. Many young painters took heart from Steinberg's opposition to the idea that formalist criteria were the only means for judging content, and his challenge to the reductivist simplifications of recent art criticism. A few times a week I talked to Tom Hess, who loved painting as I did; when Tom died, I mainly talked to myself.

Last year, I began to see a lot of painters again. There was no Club, no forum, no bar, no school, no magazine they congregated around, but there were four critical exhibitions that took place in 1978-79, where painters gathered: Cézanne, The Late Works, Monet at Giverny, the Jasper Johns retrospective and Abstract Expressionism: The Formative Years. The cumulative effect of these exhibitions was a giant shot in the arm for painting. Both the Monet and the Cézanne shows concentrated on the old age of the artist, emphasizing synthesis rather than innovation. The Johns retrospective showed the work of a painter who rejected the facile iconography of Pop Art to paint (with oil and brushes on rectangular stretched canvas!) a personal subjective vision, a world of psychologically charged images and painterly surfaces. In reality as alone as Cézanne at Aix, Johns' media persona contrasts sharply with the difficult, hermetic images he has produced since 1960, when his art began to turn around in conscious opposition to all that was winning critical praise. For Johns maintained a commitment to hand painting, fine craft, visible brushwork, subjective imagery, representation and painterly tactile surfaces for the two decades when automatic techniques, stained color field abstraction and optical art were claimed to be the only hope for high art. His refusal either to become a creature of the media or to capitulate to the one-note aesthetics of those who damned him as a "minor master" indebted to a dead European tradition were interpreted by many younger painters as exemplary negations. They saw his retrospective as the record of an artist who had continued to evolve — slowly, painstakingly, resisting the temptation to join any group — standing his solitary ground.

For younger American painters, however, struggling for over a decade to forge individual styles, the greatest revelation was exposure to the early work of the Abstract Expressionists. These extraordinary paintings, out of sight, for the most part, for thirty years, revealed the distinctively European roots of the New York School, as well as to earlier American abstraction of the Stieglitz school, which later criticism and chauvinistic packaging — sometimes by the artists themselves — conspired to obscure. Seeing what Still, Pollock, and de Kooning were doing at their age encouraged a generation of painters now mainly in their thirties to make their own mistakes, to risk failure with bold moves. Further revelations were the painterly early works of Tomlin, Krasner, Reinhardt, and Pousette-Dart, and the extent to which Motherwell, Newman, Gottlieb, Baziotes and Rothko were indebted to Surrealism. In addition, the emergence of Gorky as the great figure of the early forties contributed to a reappraisal of nature as the inspiration of lyrical painting. The refinement, nuance and technical skill of Gorky's exquisite works reaffirmed a commitment to painting as a sensual, tactile experience involving hand as well as eye and brain.

Although I stopped writing about contemporary art, I continued to find provocative, if not yet fully mature work, in studios, and even occasionally in galleries run by adventurous young dealers like Paula Cooper, Klaus Kertess, Michael Walls, Mary Boone, Miani Johnson and Patricia Hamilton. After many years of watching with interest the development of this work, I suddenly began to see in 1979, in studio after studio, bold and affirmative images executed with a new degree of complexity, density, assurance and ambition. Dozens of artists had begun simultaneously to "break through" — not to some radical technique or bizarre material — but to their own personal images. I found these artists not through galleries, museums, or art magazines, but through the artists' grapevine, the underground signalling system that has proved an infallibly accurate barometer of a change in the weather. What I have seen is obviously not all there is to see of quality and originality, but to find so much of a high calibre was enough to give me the courage and the incentive to write again about contemporary art.

Barbara Rose
New York, New York

AMERICAN PAINTING: THE EIGHTIES

*You know exactly what I think about
photography. I would like to see it make people
despise painting until something else will make
photography unbearable.*
    — *Marcel Duchamp, Letter to Alfred Stieglitz, May 17, 1922*
    (Beinecke Library, Yale)

*To hold that one kind of art must invariably be
superior or inferior to another kind means to
judge before experiencing; and the whole history
of art is there to demonstrate the futility of rules
of preference laid down beforehand: the
impossibility, that is, of anticipating the outcome
of aesthetic experience . . .*
*. . . connoisseurs of the future may be able, in
their discourse, to distinguish and name more
aspects of quality in the Old Masters, as well as in
abstract art, than we can. And in doing these
things they may find much more common ground
between the Old Masters and abstract art than we
ourselves can yet recognize.*
    — *Clement Greenberg,*
    "Abstract, Representational and so forth," 1954

Ten years ago, the question, "Is painting
dead?" was seriously being raised as artist after
artist deserted the illusory world of the canvas
for the "real" world of three-dimensional
objects, performances in actual time and space,
or the second-hand duplication of reality in
mechanically reproduced images of video, film
and photography. The traditional activity of
painting, especially hand painting with brush
on canvas, as it had been practiced in the West
since oil painting replaced manuscript illumina-
tion and frescoed murals, seemed to offer no
possibility for innovation, no potential for
novelty so startling it could compete with the
popular culture for attention, with the capacity
of the factory for mass production, or the
power of political movements to make history
and change men's minds. In the context of the
psychedelic sixties and the post-Viet Nam
seventies, painting seemed dwarfed and dimin-
ished compared with what was going on
outside the studio. In the past, of course, the
painter would never have compared his activity

with the practical side of life; but by the time
Senator Javits presented President Kennedy
with an American flag painted by Jasper Johns,
the idea that art was an activity parallel in some
way with politics, business, technology and
entertainment was on the way to becoming a
mass delusion.

Once Andy Warhol not only painted the
headlines, but appeared in them as well, the
potential parity of the artist with the pop star or
the sports hero was stimulating the drive to
compete instilled in every American by our
educational system. In the past, a painter might
compete with the best of his peers, or in the
case of the really ambitious and gifted, with the
Old Masters themselves; but now, the cele-
brated dissolution of the boundary between art
and life compelled the artist to compete with
the politician for power, with the factory for
productivity, and with pop culture for sensation
and novelty.

Perhaps most pernicious, the drive toward
novelty, which began to seem impossible to
attain within the strictly delimitative conventions of easel painting, was further encouraged
by the two dominant critical concepts of the
sixties and seventies: the first was the idea that
quality was in some way inextricably linked to
or even a by-product of innovation; the second
was that since quality was not definable, art
only needed to be interesting instead of good.
These two crudely positivistic formulations of
critical criteria did more to discourage serious
art and its appreciation than any amount of
indifference in the preceding decades. The
definition of quality as something that required
verification to give criticism its authority contributed to the identification of quality with
innovation. For if quality judgments had any
claim to objectivity, they had to be based on
the idea that an artist did something *first* — an
historical fact that could be verified through
documentation. The further erosion of critical
authority was accomplished in other quarters
by the denial that quality was in any way a
transcendent characteristic of the art work; for
if a work validated its existence primarily by
being "interesting" (i.e. novel), then qualitative

distinctions were no longer necessary. Far more aligned than they might appear at first, these two materialist critical positions conspired to make painting less than it had ever been, to narrow its horizons to the vanishing point.

Thus, in the sixties and seventies, criticism militated on two fronts against styles that were based on continuity instead of rupture with an existing tradition. The term "radical" vied with "advanced" as the greatest accolade in the critic's vocabulary. Slow-moving, painstaking tortoises were outdistanced by swift hares, hopping over one another to reach the finish line where painting disappeared into nothingness. Such an eschatological interpretation of art history was the inevitable result of the pressure to make one's mark through innovation; for those who could not be first, at least there was the possibilty of being the first to be last.

I. REDUCING RECIPES

This drive toward reductivism, encouraged and supported by a rigorously positivist criticism that outlawed any discussions of content and metaphor as belonging to the unspeakable realm of the ineffable, was a surprising finale to Abstract Expressionism, which had begun with an idealistic Utopian program for preserving not only the Western tradition of painting, but also the entire Graeco-Roman system of moral and cultural values. Of course this was to ask of art more than art could deliver; the revulsion against such rhetoric was a primary reason for the rejection of Abstract Expressionist aesthetics by pop and minimal artists beginning around 1960.

To be accurate, however, one must recall that the subversion of Abstract Expressionism began within the ranks of the movement itself. A popular art world joke described the demise of "action painting" as follows: Newman closed the window, Rothko pulled down the shade, and Reinhardt turned out the lights. A gross over-simplification of the critique of gestural styles by these three absolutist artists, this pithy epithet indicates the superficial manner that the works of Newman, Rothko and Reinhardt were interpreted by art students throughout America, anxious to take their places in the limelight and the art market, without traveling the full distance of the arduous route that transformed late Abstract Expressionism into simplified styles subsuming elements from earlier modern movements into a synthesis that while reductive, was still a synthesis. What lay behind Abstract Expressionism was forgotten ancient history in the art schools, where recipes for instant styles (two tablespoons Reinhardt, one half-cup Newman, a dash of Rothko with Jasper Johns frosting was a favorite) pressed immature artists into claiming superficial trademarks. These styles in turn were authenticated by art historians trained only in modern art history, and quickly exported to Europe, where World War II and its aftermath had created an actual historical rupture and an anxiety to catch up and overtake American art by starting out with the *dernier cri.* Soon the minimal, monochromatic styles that imitated Newman, Rothko and Reinhardt in a way no less shameless than the manner de Kooning's Ten Street admirers copied the look of his works, gave a bad name to good painting on both sides of the Atlantic.

Yet more disastrous in its implications was the haste to find a recipe for instant innovation in Pollock's complex abstractions. Not well represented in New York museums, rarely seen in the provinces at all, these daring works were essentially known through reproduction and in the widely diffused photographs and films Hans Namuth made of Pollock at work. The focus on Pollock as a performer in action rather than as a contemplative critic of his own work and student of the Old Masters — which was closer to the truth — meshed perfectly with the American proclivity to act first, think later. With little or no idea of what had gone into the making of Pollock's so-called "drip" paintings, which vaulted him into international celebrity as the last artist to genuinely *épater le bourgeois,* young artists turned to Happenings, the "theater of action", and other forms of public performance. Later, Namuth's photographs, which made the liquid paint look solid, promoted a series of random "distributional" pieces of materials poured, dropped or dumped on the floor of museums and galleries. These ephemera signaled the end of minimal art in a misguided attempt to literalize Pollock's "drip" paintings in actual space.

This is not to say that all the artists of the sixties and seventies who interpreted Abstract Expressionism literally — seizing on those aspects of the works of the New York School that seemed most unlike European art — were cynical or meretricious. But they were hopelessly provincial. And it is as provincial that most of the art of the last two decades is likely to be viewed when the twentieth century is seen in historical perspective. By provincial, I mean art that is determined predominantly by topical references in reaction to local concerns, to the degree that it lacks the capacity to transcend inbred national habits of mind to express a universal truth. In the sixties and seventies, the assertion of a specifically American consciousness was an objective to be pursued instead of avoided. The Abstract Expressionists by and large had European or immigrant backgrounds; they rejected the strictly "American" expression as an impediment to universality. Beginning around 1960, however, the pursuit of a distinctively American art by native-born artists provided the rationale for the variety of puritanically precise and literalist styles that have dominated American art since Abstract Expressionism. A reductive literalism became the aesthetic credo; the characteristics of painting as mute object were elevated over those of painting as illusion or allusion.

II. TECHNIQUE AS CONTENT

Even those artists who maintained closer contact with the European tradition, like Bannard and Olitski, avoiding the provincial American look, were unable to find more in painting than left-overs from the last banquet of the School of Paris, art informel. However, tachiste art, with its emphasis on materials, was nearly as literal as the local American styles. The absence of imagery in Yves Klein's monochrome "blue" paintings, the ultimate informel works, identifies content not with imagery or pictorial structure, but with technique and materials. In identifying image and content with materials, informel styles coincided with the objective literalist direction of American painting after Abstract Expressionism.

The identification of content with technique and materials rather than image, however, also had its roots in Abstract Expressionism. In seeking an alternative to Cubism, the Abstract Expressionists, influenced by the Surrealists, came to believe that formal invention was primarily to be achieved through technical innovation. To some extent, this was true; automatic procedures contributed in large measure to freeing the New York School from Cubist structure, space and facture. But once these automatic processes were divorced from their image-creating function, in styles that disavowed drawing as a remnant of the dead European past to be purged, the absence of imagery threw the entire burden of pictorial expression on the intrinsic properties of materials. The result was an imageless, or virtually imageless, abstract painting as fundamentally materially oriented as the literal "object art" it purported to oppose.

The radicality of object art consisted of converting the plastic elements of illusion in painting — i.e. light, space and scale — into actual properties lacking any imaginative, subjective or transcendental dimension. No intercession by the imagination was required to infer them as realities because they were a priori "real". This conversion of what was illusory in painting into literal realities corresponds specifically to the process of reification. As the fundamental characteristic of recent American art, anti-illusionism reveals the extent to which art, in the service of proclaiming its "reality", has ironically been further alienated from the life of the imagination. The reductio *ad absurdem* of this tendency to make actual what in the past had been a function of the imagination was so-called "process art", which illustrated the procedure of gestural painting, without committing itself to creating images of any permanence that would permit future judgment. In conceptual art, the further reification of criticism was undertaken by minds too impotent to create art, too terrified to be judged, and too ambitious to settle for less than the status of the artist.

Thus it was in the course of the past two decades that first the criticism, and then the art that reduced it to formula and impotent theory, became so detached from sensuous experience that the work of art itself could ultimately be conceived as superfluous to the art activity — which by now epitomized precisely that alienation and reification it nominally critized. Such were the possibilities of historical contradiction in the "revolutionary" climate of the sixties and seventies. In painting, or what remained of it, a similar process of reification of the illusory was undertaken. Edge had to be literal and not drawn so as not to suggest illusion; shape and structure had to coincide with one another to proclaim themselves as suffcently "real" for painting to satisfy the requirements of radicality. In reducing painting to nothing other or more than its material components, rejecting all forms of illusionism as *retardataire* and European, radical art was forced to renounce any kind of illusive or allusive imagery simply to remain radical. And it was as *radical* that the ambitious artist felt compelled to identify himself. In its own terms, the pursuit of radicality was a triumph of positivism; the rectangular colored surface inevitably became an object as literal as the box in the room. Even vestigial allusions of landscape in the loaded surface style that evolved from stained painting in gelled, cracked or coagulated pigment — reminiscent of Ernst's experiments with decalcomania — express a nostalgia for meaning, rather than any convincing metaphor. For radicality demanded that imagery, presumably dependent on the outmoded conventions of representational art, was to be avoided at all costs. The result of such a wholesale rejection of imagery, which cut across the lines from minimal to color-field painting in recent years, was to create a great hunger for images. This appetite was gratified by the art market with photography and Photo-Realism.

III. AGAINST PHOTOGRAPHY

Photography and the slick painting styles related to it answered the appetite for images; but they did so at the enormous price of sacrificing all the sensuous, tactile qualities of surface, as well as the metaphorical and metaphysical aspects of imagery that it is the unique capacity of painting to deliver. Pop art, which is based on reproduced images, had self-consciously mimicked the impersonal surfaces of photography, but Photo-Realism rejected this ironic distance and aped the documentary image without embarrassment. In a brilliant analysis of the limitations of photograph, ("What's All This About Photography?" *ARTFORUM,* Vol. 17, No. 9, May, 1979) painter Richard Hennessy defines the crucial differences between photographic and pictorial imagery. A devastating argument against photography ever being other than a minor art because of its intrinsic inability to transcend reality, no matter what its degree of abstraction, the article makes a compelling case for the necessity of painting, not only as an expressive human activity, but also as our only present hope for preserving major art, since the subjugation of sculpture and architecture to economic concerns leaves only painting genuinely "liberal" in the sense of free.

According to Hennessy, photography, and by inference, painting styles derived from it, lacks surface qualities, alienating it from sensuous experience. More than any of the so-called optical painting styles, photography truly addresses itself to eyesight alone. Upon close inspection, the detail of photography breaks down into a uniform chemical film — that is, into something other than the image it records — in a way that painterly detail, whether an autonomous abstract stroke, or a particle of legible representation as in the Old Masters, does not. Thus it is the visible record of the activity of the human hand, as it builds surfaces experienced as tactile, that differentiates painting from mechanically reproduced imagery. (Conversely, the call for styles that are exclusively *optical* may indicate a critical taste unconsciously influenced in its preference by daily commerce with the opticality of reproduced images.)

The absence of the marks of the human hand that characterizes the detached automatic techniques of paint application with spraygun, sponge, spilling, mopping and screening typical of recent American painting, relates it to graphic art as well as to mechanical reproductions that are stamped and printed.

IV. EXAMPLE OF HOFMANN

Among the first painters to insist on a "maximal" art that is sensuous, tactile, imagistic, metaphorical and subjective, Hennessy himself painted in a variety of styles, examining the means and methods of the artists he most admired — Picasso, Matisse, Klee, Miró, and above all Hans Hofmann. The latter has come to symbolize for many younger painters the courage to experiment with different styles, to mature late, after a long career of assimilating elements from the modern movements in a synthesis that is inclusive and not reductive. Indeed, Hofmann's commitment to preserving all that remained alive in the Western tradition of painting, while rejecting all that was worn out by convention or superseded by more complex formulation, has become the goal of the courageous and ambitious painters today.

Who could have predicted in 1966, when Hofmann, teacher of the Abstract Expressionists, who brought Matisse's and Kandinsky's principles to New York, died in his eighties, that the late-blooming artist would become the model for those ready to stake their lives on the idea that painting had not died with him? Hofmann's example was important in many

ways, for he had remained throughout his life an easel painter, untempted by the architectural aspirations of the "big picture" that dwarfed the viewer in its awesome environmental expanse. Conscious of allover design, Hofmann nevertheless chose to orient his paintings in one direction, almost aways vertically, the position that parallels that of the viewer. The vertical orientation, which implies confrontation, rather than the domination of the viewer by the painting, is also typical of many of the artists of the eighties, who accept the conventions of easel painting as a discipline worthy of preservation. Moreover, Hofmann had also turned his back on pure automatism, after early experiments with dripping. Like Hofmann, with few exceptions, the artists who follow his example, maintain that painting is a matter of an image that is frontal and based on human scale relationships. They paint on the wall, on stretched canvases that are roughly life-size, working often from preliminary drawings, using brushes or palette knives that record the marks of personal involvement and hand craft, balancing out spatial tensions by carefully revising, as Hofmann did.

Of course, not all the artists I am speaking of have a specific debt to Hofmann. In fact, the serious painters of the eighties are an extremely heterogeneous group — some abstract, some representational. But they are united on a sufficient number of critical issues that it is possible to isolate them as a group. They are, in the first place, dedicated to the preservation of painting as a transcendental high art, a major art, and an art of universal as opposed to local or topical significance. Their aesthetic, which synthesizes tactile with optical qualities, defines itself in conscious opposition to photography and all forms of mechanical reproduction which seek to deprive the art work of its unique "aura". It is, in fact, the enhancement of this aura, through a variety of means, that painting now self-consciously intends — either by emphasizing the involvement of the artist's hand, or by creating highly individual visionary images that cannot be confused either with reality itself or with one another. Such a commitment to unique images necessarily rejects seriality as well.

V. THE PAINTER AS IMAGE MAKER

These painters will probably find it odd, and perhaps even disagreeable, since they are individualists of the first order, to be spoken of as a group, especially since for the most part they are unknown to one another. However, all are equally committed to a distinctively humanistic art that defines itself in opposition to the *a priori* and the mechanical: A machine cannot do it, a computer cannot reproduce it, another artist cannot execute it. Nor does their painting in any way resemble prints, graphic art, advertising, billboards, etc. Highly and consciously structured in its final evolution (often after a long process of being refined in preliminary drawings and paper studies), these paintings are clearly the works of rational adult humans, not a monkey, a child, or a lunatic. Here it should be said that although there is a considerable amount of painting that continues Pop Art's mockery of reproduced images — some of it extremely well done — there is a level of cynicism, sarcasm and parody in such work that puts it outside the realm of high art, placing it more properly in the context of caricature and social satire.

The imagery of painters committed exclusively to a tradition of painting, an inner world of stored images ranging from Altamira to Pollock, is entirely invented; it is the product exclusively of the individual imagination rather than a mirror of the ephemeral external world of objective reality. Even when such images are strictly geometric, as in the case of artists like Susanna Tanger, Lenny Contino, Peter Pinchbeck, Elaine Cohen, Georges Noel and Robert Feero, they are quirky and sometimes eccentrically personal interpretations of geometry — always asymmetrical or skewed, implying a dynamic and precarious balance, the opposite of the static immobility of the centered icon, emblem or insignia. The rejection of symmetry and of literal interpretations of "allover" design, such as the repeated motifs of Pattern Painting, defines this art as exclusively *pictorial;* it is as unrelated to the repetitious motifs of the decorative arts and the static centeredness of ornament as it is to graphics and photography. For the rejection of the encroachments made on painting by the minor arts is another of the defining characteristics of the serious painting of the eighties.

Although these artists refuse to literalize any of the elements of painting, including that of "allover" design, some, like Howard Buchwald, Joan Thorne, Nancy Graves and Mark Schlesinger are taking up the challenge of Pollock's allover paintings in a variety of ways without imitating Pollock's image. Buchwald, for example, builds up a strong rhythmic counterpoint of curved strokes punctuated by linear slices and ovoid sections cut through the canvas at angles and points determined by a system of perspective projections referring to space in front of, rather than behind, the picture plane. Thorne and Graves superimpose several different imagery systems, corresponding to the layers of Pollock's interwoven skeins of paint, upon one another. Schlesinger, on the other hand, refers to Pollock's antecedents in the allover stippling of Neo-Impressionism, which he converts into images of jagged-edged spiraling comets suggesting a plunge into deep space while remaining clearly on the surface by eschewing any references to value contrasts or sculptural modeling. These original and individual interpretations of "allover" structure point to the wide number of choices still available within pictorial as opposed to decorative art. For in submitting itself to the supporting role that decorative styles inevitably play in relationship to architecture, painting renounces its claims to autonomy.

VI. THE LEGACY OF POLLOCK

To a large number of these artists, Pollock's heroism was not taking the big risk of allowing much to chance, but his success in depicting a life-affirming image in an apparent state of emergence, evolution and flux — a flickering, dancing image that never permits the eye to come to rest on a single focus. Like Pollock's inspired art, some of these paintings emphasize images that seem to be in a state of evolution. Images of birth and growth like Lois Lane's bulbs, buds and hands and Susan Rothenberg's desperate animals and figures that seem about to burst the membrane of the canvas to be born before us, or Robert Moskowitz' boldly hieratic windmill that stands erect in firm but unaggressive confrontation — a profound metaphor of a man holding his ground — are powerful metaphors. In the works of Lenny Contino and Dennis Ashbaugh, as well as in Carol Engelson's processional panels, a kind of surface dazzle and optical excitement recall the energy and sheer physical exhilaration that proclaimed the underlying image of Pollock's work as the life force itself. Because he was able to create an image resonant with meaning and rich with emotional association without resorting to the conventions of representational art, Pollock remains the primary touchstone. The balance he achieved between abstract form and allusive content now appears as a renewed goal more than twenty years after Pollock's death.

As rich in its potential as Cubism, Abstract Expressionism is only now beginning to be understood in a profound instead of a superficial way. What is emerging from careful scrutiny of its achievements is that the major areas of breakthrough of the New York School were not the "big picture", automatism, action painting, flatness, et.al., but the synthesis of painting and drawing, and a new conception of figuration that freed the image from its roots in representational art. For Cubism, while fracturing, distorting and in other ways splintering the image (something neither Abstract Expressionism or the wholistic art that came from it did) could never free itself of the conventions of representational art to become fully abstract.

Drawing on discoveries that came after Pollock regarding the role of figuration in post-Cubist painting, artists today are at ease with a variety of representational possibilites that derive, not from Cubist figuration, but from the continuity of image with surface established by Still, Rothko, Newman and Reinhardt, who imbedded, so to speak, the figure in the carpet, in such a way as to make figure and field covalent and coextensive.

In the current climate of carefully considered re-evaluation, the rejection of figure-ground relationships, which artists of the sixties labelled as superannuated conventions inherited from Cubism, is being reviewed and reformulated in more subtle and less brutal terms. Cutting the figure out of the ground to eliminate the recession of shapes behind the plane was an instant short-cut solution to a complex problem. Ripping the figure from the ground eliminated figure-ground discontinuities in a typically Duchampesque solution of negating the problem. (Interestingly, Johns, usually considered Duchamp's direct heir, backed off from the objectness of the *Flag,* in which he identified image with field, and found another solution to reconciling representation with flatness by embedding the figure in the ground in later works such as *Flag on Orange Field.)*

Short-cuts, recipes, textbook theorizing and instant solutions to difficult problems are being rejected today as much as trademarks and the mass-produced implications of seriality. Today, subtler modes of dealing with the relationship between image and ground without evoking Cubist space are being evolved. Even artists like Carl Apfelschnitt, Sam Gilliam and Ron Gorchov, who alter the shape of the stretcher somewhat, do so not to identify their paintings as virtual objects, but to amplify the meaning of imagery. Apfelschnitt and Gorchov, for example, make totemic images whose sense of presence relies on metaphorical associations with shields and archaic devices; Gilliam bevels the edge of his rectangular canvas to permit freer play to his landscape illusion, insuring that his dappled Impressionism cannot be interpreted as the naive illusion of a garden through a window.

VII. POST-CUBIST REPRESENTATION

The difficulties of reconciling figuration, the mode of depicting images whether abstract or representational, with post-Cubist space has been resolved by these painters in a variety of ways. Precedents for post-Cubist representation exist in Pollock's black-and-white paintings, and more recently in Guston's figurative style. Drawing directly in paint, as opposed to using drawing as a means to contour shape, has given a new freedom to artists like Nancy Graves, Richard Hennessy, William Ridenhour, Anna Bialobroda, Steven Sloman and Luisa Chase. In that post-Cubist representation is not based on an abstraction from the external objective world, but on self-generated images, it is a mental construct as conceptual in origin as the loftiest non-objective painting. Lacking any horizon line, Susan Rothenberg's white-on-white horse, Lois Lane's black-on-black tulips, and Robert Moskowitz' red-on-red windmill, or Gary Stephan's brown-on-brown torso have more in common with Malevich's *White-on-White* or Reinhardt's black crosses in black fields than with any realist painting. Like Dubuffet's *Cows* — perhaps the first example of post-Cubist representation — and Johns' targets and numbers, these images are visually embedded in their fields, whose surface they continue. This contiguity between image and field, enhanced by an equivalence of facture in both, identifies image and field with the surface plane in a manner that is convincingly modernist.

The possibility of depicting an image without resorting to Cubist figure-ground relationships greatly enlarges the potential of modernist painting for the future. No longer does the painter who wishes to employ the full range of pictorial possibilities have to choose between a reductivist suicide or a retrenchment back to realism. By incorporating discoveries regarding the potential for figuration with an abstract space implicit in Monet, Matisse, and Miró, as this potential was refined by Pollock and the color-field painters, an artist may choose a representational style that is not realist.

Today, it is primarily in their pursuit of legible, stable, imagistic styles — both abstract and representational — structured as indivisible wholes (another legacy of color-field painting) rather than composed in the traditional Cubist manner of adding on parts that rhyme and echo one another that modernist painters are united. Even those who make use of loosely geometric structures for painterly brushwork like Mark Lancaster, Pete Omlor and Pierre Haubensak, do so in a highly equivocal way that does not allude to Cubic figure-ground inversions, but rather recalls Impressionist and Fauve integrations of the figure into the ground. Their images suggest poetic associations with the grid of windows, a play on the illusion of the picture as window; but they do not pretend in any way that the picture *is* in any way a window. Still others, like Thornton Willis, Vered Lieb, Susan Crile, and Frances Barth, are even freer in their use of geometry as a structuring container for color, rather than as a rigid *a priori* category of ideal forms.

In all of these cases, the representation of an image never invokes naive illusionism; to remain valid as a modernist concept, figuration is rendered compatible with flatness. This may mean nothing more radical than Clive Bell's assumption that a painting must proclaim itself as such before it is a woman, a horse or a sunrise, or Serusier's definition of a painting as a flat surface covered with patches of color. However, it does necessitate conveying the information that the depicted image is incontrovertibly two-dimensional, that it lies on the plane, and not behind it. The contiguity of image with ground is established often as the Impressionists did, by an allover rhythmic stroking. All that in Cubism remained as vestigial references to the representational past of painting — value contrast, modeling, perspective, overlapping, receding planes, etc. — is eliminated so that the space of painting cannot be confused with real space. Once the truth of the illusion of painting — and *illusion, not flatness, is the essence of painting* — the artist is free to manipulate and transform imagery into all manner of illusions belonging exclusively to the realm of the pictorial, i.e., the realm of the imagination. Moreover, since the depicted illusions belong to the imagination, i.e., they are registered by the brain and the eye. Surface, perceived as constituted of pigment on canvas can be manipulated to evoke a tactile response that has nothing to do with the experience of a third dimension, but is entirely a matter of texture.

The difference between a painting that is composed, a process of addition and subtraction, and one that is constructed, through a structuring process that takes into consideration the architecture of the frame, continues to be a primary consideration. These artists take a responsibility to structure for granted, just as they reject the random, the chance and the automatic as categories of the irresponsible. In this sense, decision-making, the process of deliberation, becomes a moral as well as an aesthetic imperative.

Sifting through the modern movements, panning the gold and discarding the dross, the painters of the eighties, as we have seen, retain much from Abstract Expressionism. In many cases, there is a commitment to a kinetic or visceral metaphor. However, this appeal to empathy in the energetic and muscular images of Elizabeth Murray, Dennis Ashbaugh, Stewart Hitch, Georges Noel, Howard Buchwald, Robert Feero and Joane Thorne, or in the movement implied by Susan Rothenberg, Edward Youkilis and Joanna Mayor, has more in common with the "life-enhancing" quality Bernard Berenson identified as our empathic identification with Signorelli's nudes than with the documentary and autobiographical gestures of "action painting".

VIII. THE FUNCTION OF THE IMAGINATION

Today, the essence of painting is being redefined not as a narrow, arid and reductive anti-illusionism, but as a rich, varied capacity to birth new images into an old world. The new generation of painters who have matured slowly, skeptically, privately, and with great difficulty, have had to struggle to maintain conviction in an art that the media and the museums said was dying. Today, it is not the literal material properties of painting as pigment on cloth, but its capacity to materialize an image, not behind the picture plane, which self-awareness proclaims inviolate, but behind the proverbial looking-glass of consciousness, where the depth of the imagination knows no limits. If an illusion of space is evoked, it is simultaneously rescinded. In one way or another, either in terms of Hofmann's "push-pull" balancing out of pictorial tensions, or by calling attention to the actual location of the plane by emphasizing the physical build-up of pigment on top of it, or by embedding the figure into its contiguous field, serious painting today does not ignore the fundamental assumptions of modernism, which precludes any regression to the conventions of realist representation.

Not innovation, but originality, individuality and synthesis are the marks of quality in art today, as they have always been. Not material flatness — in itself a contradiction, since even thin canvas has a third dimension and any mark on it creates space — but the capacity of painting to evoke, imply and conjure up magical illusions that exist in an imaginative mental space, which like the atmospheric space of a Miró, a Rothko or a Newman, or the cosmic space of a Kandinsky or a Pollock, cannot be confused with the tangible space outside the canvas, is that which differentiates painting from the other arts and from the everyday visual experiences of life itself.

The idea that painting is somehow a visionary and not a material art, and that the locus of its inspiration is in the artist's subjective unconscious was the crucial idea that Surrealism passed on to Abstract Expressionism. After two decades of the rejection of imaginative poetic fantasy for the purportedly greater "reality" of an objective art based exclusively on verifiable fact, the current rehabilitation of the metaphorical and metaphysical implications of imagery is a validation of a basic Surrealist insight. The liberating potential of art is not as literal reportage, but as a catharsis of the imagination.

The Surrealists believed, and no one has yet proved them wrong, that psychic liberation is the prerequisite of political liberation, and not vice-versa. For most of the twentieth century, the relationship between art and politics has been an absurd confusion, sometimes comic, sometimes tragic. The idea that to be valid or important art must be "radical" is at the heart of this confusion. By aspiring to power, specifically political power, art imitates the compromises of politics and renounces its essential role as moral example. By turning away from power and protest, by making of their art a moral example of mature responsibility and judicious reflection, a small group of painters "taking a stand within the self", as Ortega y Gasset described Goethe's morality, is redeeming for art a high place in culture that recent years have seen it voluntarily abdicate for the cheap thrill of instant impact.

Because the creation of individual, subjective images, ungoverned and ungovernable by any system of public thought or political exigency, is *ipso facto* revolutionary and subversive of the status quo, it is a tautology that art must strive to be radical. On the contrary, that art which commits itself self-consciously to radicality — which usually means the technically and materially radical, since only technique and not the content of the mind advances — is a mirror of the world as it is and not a critique of it.

Even Herbert Marcuse was forced to revise the Marxist assumption that in the perfect Utopian society, art would disappear. In his last book, *The Aesthetic Dimension,* he concludes that even an unrepressed, unalienated world "would not signal the end of art, the overcoming of tragedy, the reconciliation of the Dionysian and the Apollonian . . . In all its ideality, art bears witness to the truth of dialectical materialism — the permanent non-identity between subject and object, individual and individual." Marcuse identifies the only truly revolutionary art as the expression of subjectivity, the private vision:

"The 'flight into inwardness' and the insistence on a private sphere may well serve as bulwarks against a society which administers all dimensions of human existence. Inwardness and subjectivity may well become the inner and outer space for the subversion of experience, for the emergence of another universe."

For art, the patricidal act of severing itself from tradition and convention is equally suicidal, the self-hatred of the artist expressed in eliminating the hand, typical of the art of the last two decades, can only lead to the death of painting. Such a powerful wish to annihilate personal expression implies that the artist does not love his creation. And it is obvious that an activity practiced not out of love, but out of competition, hatred, protest, the need to dominate materials, institutions or other people, or simply to gain social status in a world that canonizes as well as cannibalizes the artist, is not only alienated but doomed. For art is labor, physical human labor, the labor of birth, reflected in the many images that appear as in a process of emergence, as if taking form before us.

The renewed conviction in the future of painting on the part of a happy few signals a shift in values. Instead of trying to escape from history, there is a new generation of artists ready to confront the past without succumbing to nostalgia, ready to learn without imitating, courageous enough to create works for a future no one can be sure will come, ready to take their place, as Gorky put it, in the chain of continuity of "the great group dance."

This is a generation of hold-outs, a generation of survivors of catastrophes, both personal and historical, which are pointless to enumerate, since their art depends on transcending the petty personal soap opera in the service of the grand, universal statement. They have survived a drug culture that consumed many of the best talents of their time; they have lived through a crisis of disintegrating morality, social demoralization and lack of conviction in all authority and tradition destroyed by cultural relativism and individual cynicism. And they have stood their ground, maintaining a conviction in quality and values, a belief in art as a mode of transcendence, a worldly incarnation of the ideal. Perhaps they, more than the generations who interpreted his lessons as license, have truly understood why Duchamp was obsessed by alchemy. Alchemy is the science of trans-substantiation; the tragedy of Duchamp's life was that he could only study alchemy because he could not practice it. To transform matter into some higher form, one must believe in transcendence. As a rationalist, a materialist and a positivist, Duchamp could not practice an art based on the transformation of physical matter into intangible energy and light. Those who perpetuate an art that filled him with ennui are the last of the true believers; their conviction in the future of painting is a courageous and constructive act of faith.

Carl Apfelschnitt

born Philadelphia, PA, 1948

Philadelphia College of Art
San Francisco Art Institute

AX-EI-EN-TA, 1979
roplex, acrisol, oil based varnish
and gold leaf on canvas, 96 x 72 inches

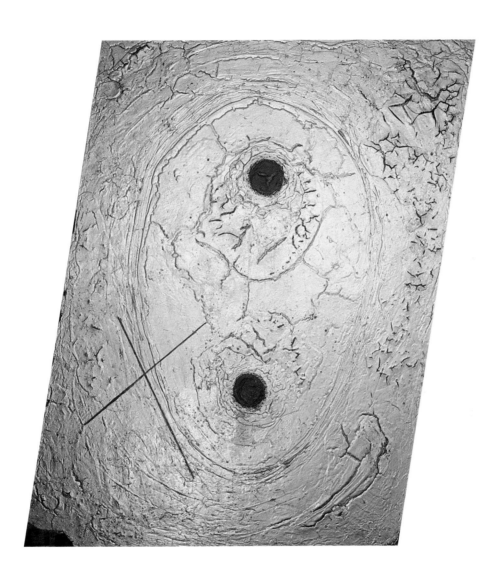

Dennis Ashbaugh

born Red Oak, Iowa, 1946

Orange Coast College
California State University
  at Fullerton

COMA-MOM, 1979
oil on canvas, 71 x 72 inches

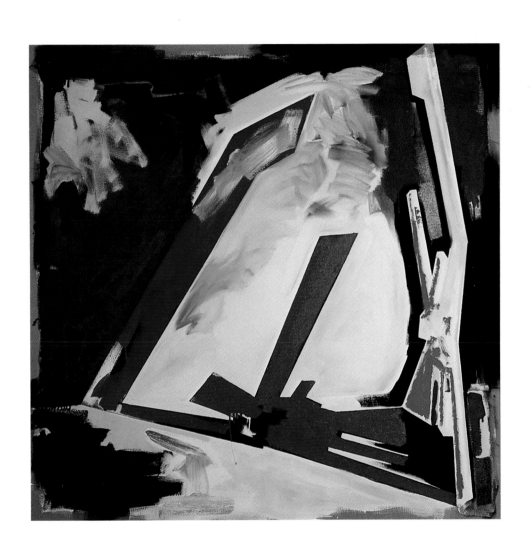

Frances Barth

born New York, NY, 1946

Hunter College

MOKROE, 1976
acrylic, pastel and charcoal on canvas,
2 panels, each 72 x 70 inches

Anna Bialobroda

born Lodz, Poland, 1946

Whitney Museum of
  American Art Study Progam
Otis Art Institute

PORTRAYAL, 1978
acrylic on canvas, 72 x 48 inches

Howard Buchwald

born New York, NY, 1943

Cooper Union
Hunter College

UNTITLED (WHEELING), 1978-79
oil on canvas, 77 x 99 inches

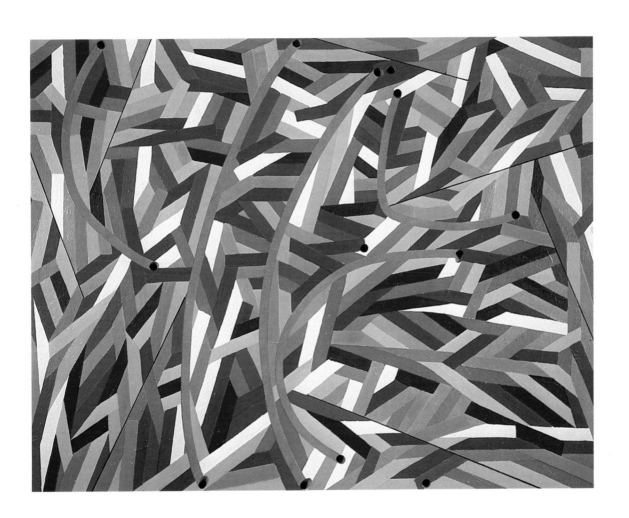

Louisa Chase

born Panama City, Panama, 1951

Syracuse University
Yale University
    Summer School of Art
Yale University
    School of Art & Architecture

OCEAN, 1979
oil on canvas, 72 x 78 inches

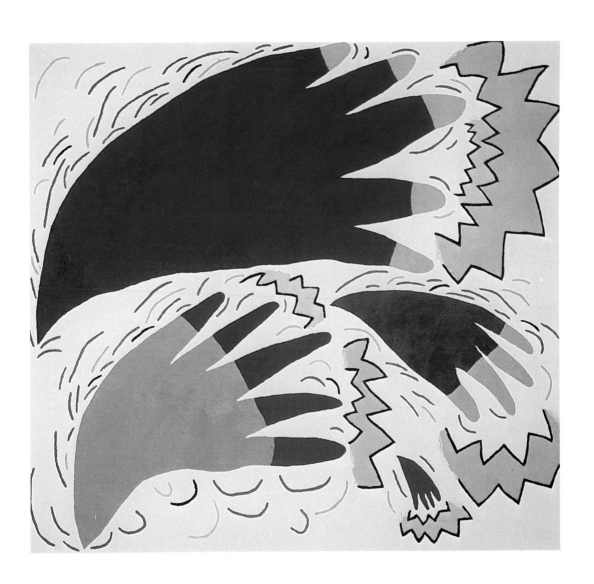

Elaine Lustig Cohen

born Jersey City, NJ, 1927

Tulane University,
    Sophie Newcomb College
University of
    Southern California

BLACK PILASTER III, 1978
acrylic on canvas, 80 x 50 inches

William Conlon

born Albany, NY, 1941

School of Visual Arts
Yale University
    School of Art & Architecture

KINDERHOOK CREEK, 1976
acrylic on canvas, 84 x 78 inches

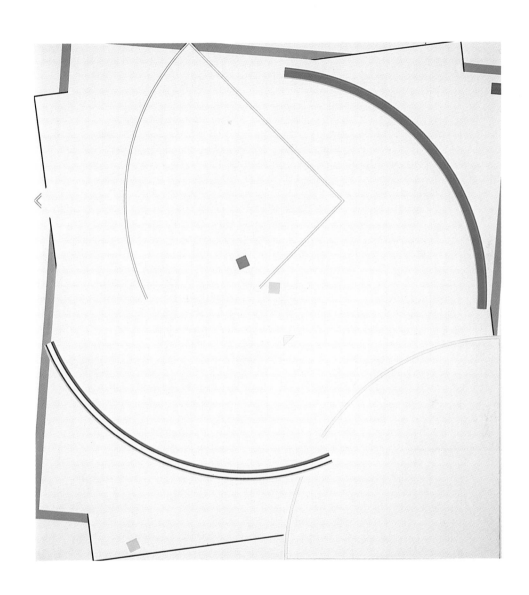

Leonard Contino

born Brooklyn, NY, 1942

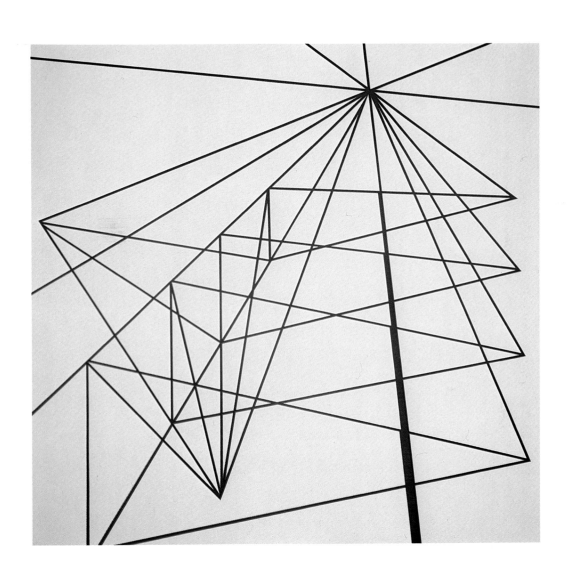

Susan Crile

born Cleveland, Ohio, 1942

New York University
Bennington College
Hunter College

TWO-FOLD, 1978
gesso and oil on canvas, 49 x 70 inches

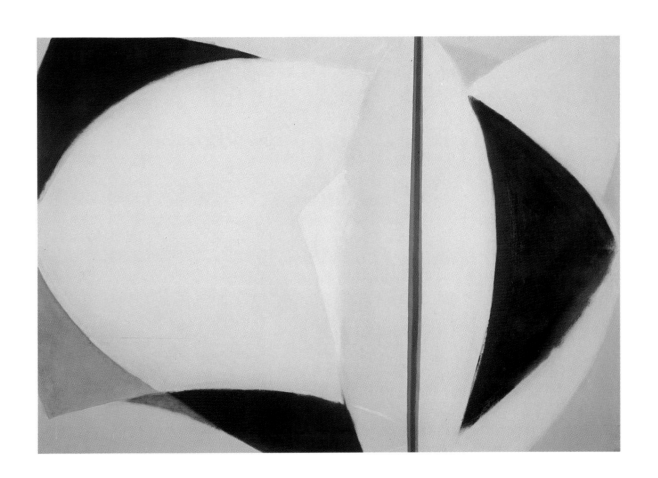

Carol Engelson

born Seymour, IN, 1944

Carnegie-Mellon University

FOR LADY ALEXANDRA NAWRUZ XXI, 1977
acrylic and oil on canvas,
6 panels, each 44 x 27 inches

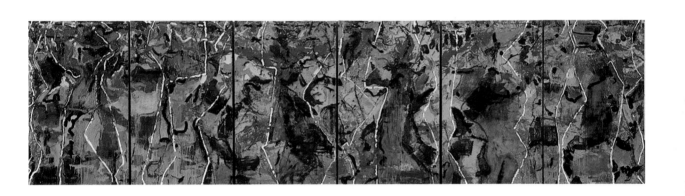

Rachelle Epstein

born New York, NY, 1947

Tyler School of Fine Art
Yale University
    School of Art & Architecture

PATTERNED AFTER A ROSE, 1979
acrylic on canvas, 80 x 71 inches

Robert Feero

born Boston, MA, 1952

Massachusetts College of Art
Whitney Museum of
    American Art Study Program
School of the Art Institute
    of Chicago

ICA, 1978
polymer on canvas, 78 x 108 inches

Hermine Ford

born New York, NY, 1939

Antioch College
Yale University
  School of Art & Architecture

RED SKY, STARS AND SHAPES FOR SUE, 1979
oil on canvas, 100 x 79 inches

Sam Gilliam

born Tupelo, MS, 1933

University of Louisville

TEQUILLA, 1979
acrylic and mixed media on canvas,
40 x 70 inches

Ron Gorchov

born Chicago, IL, 1930

University of Mississippi
Art Institute of Chicago
University of Illinois

WITCH, 1979
oil on linen, 38 x 39 inches

Nancy Graves

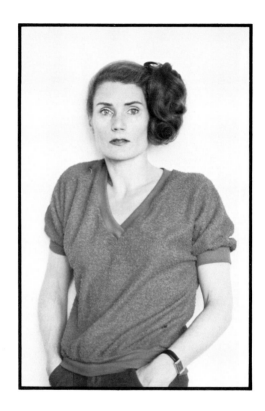

born Pittsfield, MA, 1940

Vassar College
Yale University
    School of Art & Architecture

STROBIA, 1978
oil and encaustic on canvas,
64 x 64 inches

Pierre Haubensak

born Meiringen,
   Switzerland, 1935

DERVISH, 1976
oil on canvas, 78 x 54 inches

Richard Hennessy

born Rochester, NY, 1941

Columbia University
Institute of Fine Arts, N.Y.U.

THERE WAS A GROWING AWARENESS . . ., 1978
oil on canvas, 60 x 64 inches

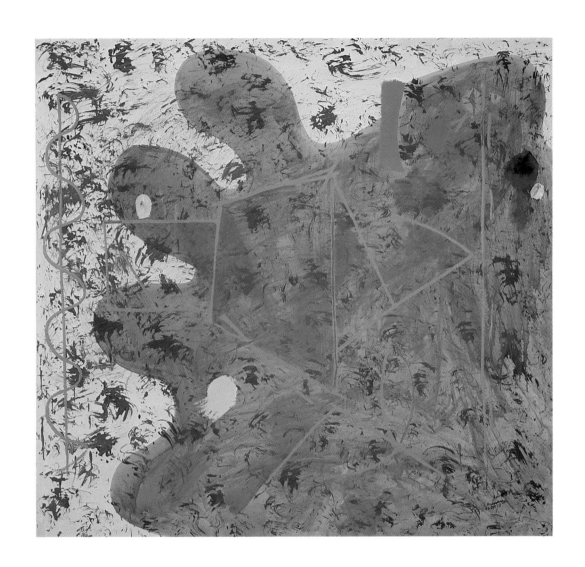

Stewart Hitch

born Lincoln, NE, 1940

University of Nebraska

Bill Jensen

born Minneapolis, MN, 1945

University of Minnesota

ANGEL, 1977
oil on linen, 36 x 24 inches

Meredith Johnson

born San Francisco, CA, 1946

California State University at
   San Francisco
Hunter College
Graduate Center, CUNY

UNTITLED, 1975
oil on canvas, 88¾ x 76 inches

Mark Lancaster

born Yorkshire, England, 1938

Bootham School, York
University of Newcastle
  upon Tyne

RED, 1974
oil on canvas, 72 x 48 inches

Lois Lane

born Philadelphia, PA, 1948

Philadelphia College of Art
Yale Summer School of
    Music and Art
Yale University
    School of Art & Architecture

UNTITLED, 1979
oil on canvas, 48 x 72 inches

Vered Lieb

born Haifa, Israel, 1947

Queens College, CUNY
Westminster College,
 Oxford, England
Arts Student League

NO ILLUSIONS, 1976
acrylic on canvas, 78 x 84 inches

Joanna Mayor

born Philadelphia, PA, 1944

Philadelphia College of Art
Pennsylvania Academy of the
   Fine Arts

UNTITLED, 1979
oil and wax on canvas, 72 x 60 inches

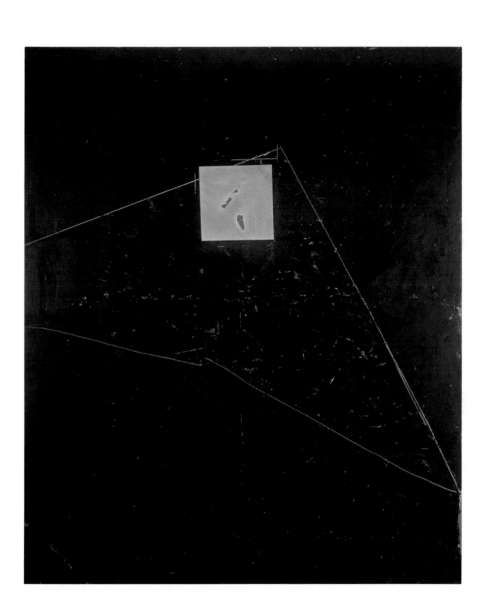

Robert Moskowitz

born New York, NY, 1935

Pratt Institute

RED MILL, 1979
oil, acrylic, latex on canvas,
108 x 63 inches

Elizabeth Murray

born Chicago, IL, 1940

Art Institute of Chicago
Mills College

FLESH EARTH & SKY, 1979
oil on canvas, 110 x 94 inches

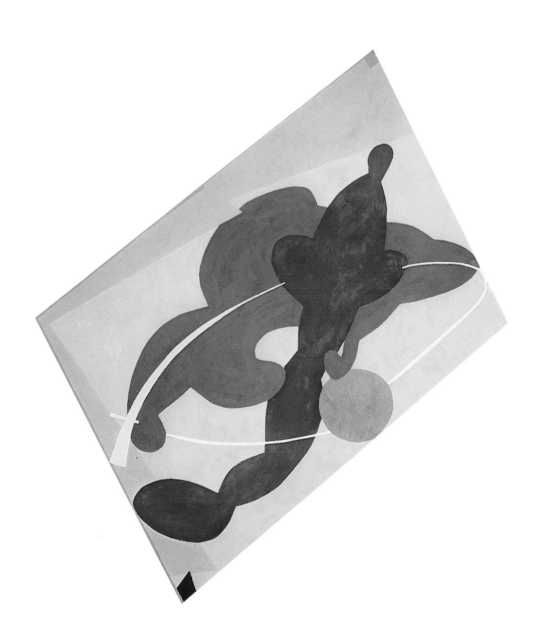

Georges Noel

born Beziers, France, 1924

Ecole Superieure, Pau, France

NEW PALIMPSESTS, 1979
acrylic on canvas, 54 x 78 inches

Pete Omlor

born Tiffin, Ohio, 1947

Cooper School of Art
Kansas City Art Institute

BUD, 1979
oil and enamel on canvas,
72 x 72 inches

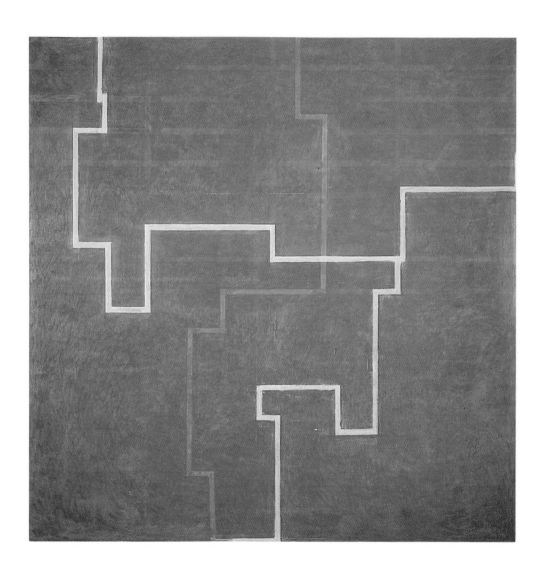

Peter Pinchbeck

born London, England, 1940

Twickenham College of Art,
  England
Polytechnic Art School,
  London, England

William Ridenhour

born Roanoke, VA, 1941

Johns Hopkins University

MISSION, 1978
acrylic on canvas, 62 x 75 inches

Susan Rothenberg

born Buffalo, NY, 1945

Cornell University
George Washington University
Corcoran Museum School

BLACK IN PLACE, 1976
acrylic and tempera on canvas,
68 x 85 inches

Mark Schlesinger

born Elizabeth, NJ, 1949

Harpur College, SUNY

ANNOUNCE, 1978-79
oil on canvas, 70 x 72 inches

Steven Sloman

born Detroit, MI, 1943

Brown University
University of Michigan
New York University
New York Studio School

LE TORSE, 1979
acrylic on canvas, 101 x 83 inches

Gary Stephan

born Brooklyn, NY, 1942

Parsons School of Design
Arts Students League
Pratt Institute
San Francisco Art Institute

HE MUST INCREASE, 1978
acrylic on canvas, 74 x 54 inches

Susanna Tanger

born Boston, MA, 1942

Boston Museum School
University of Colorado
University of California
  at Berkeley

UNTITLED, 1978
oil, rabbit skin glue on canvas,
73 x 101 inches

Joan Thorne

born Brooklyn, NY, 1943

New York University
Hunter College

EGA, 1979
oil on canvas, 76 x 67 inches

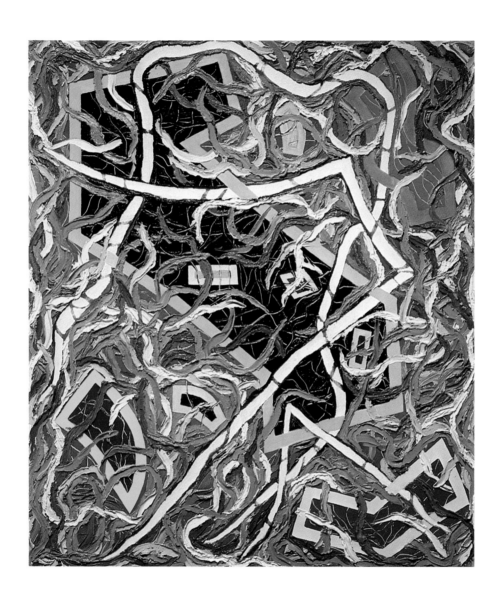

Catharine Warren

born Portland, OR, 1946

Sarah Lawrence
Academia Florence
U Torcoliere Atelier
Academie Goetz

UNTITLED, 1979
acrylic and Japanese rice paper on canvas,
2 panels, each 71 x 43 inches

Thornton Willis

born Pensacola, FL, 1936

Auburn University
University of
  Southern Mississippi
University of Alabama

BLUE SOLDIER, 1978
acrylic on canvas, 84 x 61 inches

Edward Youkilis

born Cincinnati, Ohio, 1947

Miami University, Ohio
Yale University
    School of Art & Architecture

FRAGRANT HILL, 1979
acrylic on canvas, 53 x 72 inches

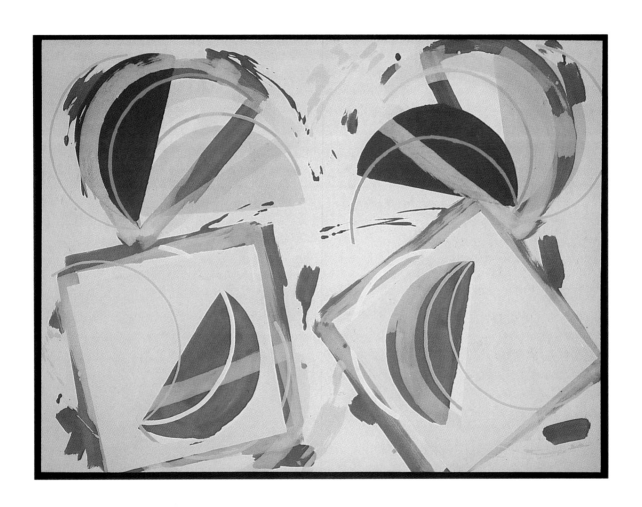

STATEMENTS

Although the artists of the eighties share a commitment to post-Cubist modernism, strong, legible images and the permanence of the Western tradition of painting, they differ on many issues, including the sources of their art and a number of technical matters, as well as on issues of interpretation. Some deal in metaphor, others do not. Some of the images are private and poetic, others public and geometric. I have made no attempt to reconcile the diversity of points of view, preferring to allow the artists to speak for themselves. Some obvious common denominators are a refreshing lack of textbook theorizing, and an appeal to the intuition and direct experience.

B.R.

Carl Apfelschnitt

I use paint to evoke a certain mythology. The imagery comes through an alternate reality. The major issue is painting as a bridge, a channel between introspective and universal visions or realities. I am altering the picture plane by deviating the traditional rectangle and using multiple layering of the surface. I approach the canvas with preconceived forms, though it is only in the process that the various elements interact to create unity.

I start with the canvas on the floor where I rub it with raw scarlet grounds mixed with Roplex #33. I don't use a brush. I pour clear Roplex #33 and Acrisol onto the painting; and alter the drying time by inscribing a shield with my hand. As this is drying, I then pour consecutive layers of pigmented Roplex #33 and retarding agent which creates stress. The vision begins to break through. On every level these surfaces agree to form relationships. The top surface agrees to crack for the bottom to come through. When I am satisfied with the surface I seal it in gold.

I want the picture plane's vibratory information to shift, to make the painting exist as an entity, synchronistically.

Dennis Ashbaugh

My work stems from previous painting and little else. I am firmly convinced that whatever contribution "contra-ceptual" art has made, its most effective mark has been to enable us to immediately identify the boring — and the insignificant. It is time for those interested in the enterprise of painting to abandon the idea that even the best Andre on the floor or a Serra on the wall has anything to do with painting.

Painting is now what it has always been about — paint, scale, color, and surface. I am only interested in full-bodied painting, all the stops pulled out, any material, any technique. My attitude towards materials and techniques is not complex. I use whatever it takes . . . linen, gesso, cheap enamel, flock, high quality oil paint, beeswax, watercolor, floor varnish, you name it. The issue is not what you use, but how to achieve full-bodied painting. The technique or the how-to is unimportant other than it gets you there. Process art taught me certain lessons. Those lessons are that in painting, procedures are never anything more than plain work, and that's not too interesting. Procedure is not art.

The conflict between abstraction and representation has never been an issue with me. Almost never do I see a figure or anything representational in say a Picasso, a Matisse, a Cézanne. However when I do see it (something representational) it always undermines and usually destroys it for me. Mondrian or Lissitsky on the other hand run the neo-plastic risk: If I notice for example just how abstract and "plastic" a painting has become (in the Mondrian sense of the word), it's shot for me.

In some ways the "1970's" did something for us all. It put us on the brink of not caring, and with few exceptions rightly so. Who could care about "a word on the wall", "a cut-off penis in Europe", "a bullet in the arm", "a white painting or even a gray painting" much less a video tape of it all. WHO CARES? Probably the same poor fools who think the 1980's is a fresh start for art. Any survey exhibition shows painfully clear that stubborn single visions are still the most interesting!

Frances Barth

Since 1969 my paintings have evolved from combinations of triangles, trapezoids, circles, implied rectangles and squares. The first structures that impressed me as a young painter were Egyptian tombs. The simplicity, grandeur, and scale of these, along with their quiet power and majesty, held a great emotive content for me. I experience the same feelings from Rothko's paintings, and from the large arabesque shapes and color of Matisse. I have always been awed by Matisse's affirmation of life. The best paintings seem to me always in the act of becoming — their time is infinite.

In his early writings, Wittgenstein said that the most important things in the world, knowledge about the world, could not be written about directly, but inferred, as by the use of parable. He referred to the works of Christ, and Tolstoy. A number of years later, a Russian formalist critic, writing about Dostoevski, said that in great literature the reader doesn't come away from the work with its formal elements impressed foremost on his mind, but more a feeling of the artist impressed on his soul. There must be an impact, presence, content, that stands beyond the materials of a work's construction.

I think it is possible in a work of art, whether abstract or representational, to have as its subject metaphor, parable, revelation. For myself I believe any work of art has to have a subject larger than its formal elements. In my own painting, I have tried to use shapes, color, space, in ways that felt like my personal language, an emotive language, that coupled with clear structure, could add up to something more than paint on a canvas.

Anna Bialobroda

Through the Western tradition and its conventions, a visual language of a constantly evolving nature was formed. This language enables artists to bring a richer knowledge to the making of abstract art today, and to establish, in their work, an ongoing dialogue based on the past wedded to the necessity of disputing it.

A painting should be a visual feast replete with the dowry of this confrontation.

Yet, in taking up the challenge of confrontation, artists must maintain a clarity of vision unimpeded by the pressures of obsolescence and technological supplantation. It is easy, in the attempt to reserve one's seat in history, to impatiently disregard the past, and hastily tout the present.

Being an abstract painter today is to have free field of a wide range of visual information, and to embrace the risk of exploring new areas of expression, thereby contributing to a finer tuning of our ever evolving visual language.

Howard Buchwald

The idea that there is a continuous tradition, a linear genealogy of change based on a model of reaction to immediately precedent works and extending forward and backward in time, no longer seems to be widely held or offer much in the way of historical explication. Partly this is because as a method it rapidly reduces to a form of historicism and is, as Meyer Schapiro has pointed out, totally inadequate as a means of explaining or justifying change.

Postures of detachment from the past are, in turn, also a totally inadequate substitute for history. An ahistorical attitude is either naive or duplicitous. It is certainly an untenable position for a painter. Painting is inherently caught up in history and tradition and this, I would argue, is its great strength and a mark of its particular relevance. Yet the rhetoric of free expression and individual spontaneity persists as does the attitude that one is free to dress up in a tradition, having chosen from a range of options, all equally valid.

The view that one chooses a tradition, besides glossing over and thereby missing the ideological mechanism of tradition, is indicative of a consumer's attitude toward the past and toward cultural production. The correlative view that one is free of tradition or the terms of history and is thrown back on one's own resources to reinvent painting (or art for that matter) out of personal feelings, unfettered by convention, is pernicious. This is nothing but willful ignorance shamming as the bourgeois notion of creativity, and is patently false.

There is within our culture a constant impetus to neutralize content, to absorb demurral and criticism through agreement, and to simplify difficult and complex issues through a leveling process which homogenizes difference. In the art world, differences manifest themselves in all manner of postures. But the divergent implications for meaning of varying positions are conveniently passed over so that no position emerges with any urgency or moral force, and in the end very little work emerges that has any necessity. This is what popularly passes for "pluralism". The specificity of particular work is blunted into useless generalities and art, losing its critical faculty, its ability to affect people's consciousness and alter their ways of thinking about the world, becomes an adjunct of entertainment.

Paintings embody a set of values through their use of specific devices and the ends toward which these devices are structured. That is, the completed painting articulates meaning and is to be taken as a sign. Paintings are meant to be read, to move away from their material and enter into discourse, but they do not usually mean to have their implicit ideological assumptions revealed. The institutional and disjunctive construction of meaning is mystified into consistency and self-adequation.

A critical view of the past is essential. It has been said that "without the past we have nothing to stand on, no context from which to organize the energies of moral vision." But for the painter, veneration of the past can be as much a problem as are the forms of cultural amnesia. The attempt on the part of artists to nostalgically align themselves with a tradition, to find support in some positive system of belief, often involves a non-critical and therefore unconscious embracing of structures and values which may be at odds with stated aims. The issue won't be forced. Painting is an utterly conventional art and conventions have social utility as well as being historically determined. One only has to acknowledge this to recognize how unnatural it is to make a painting.

Louisa Chase

Painting has become internally directed. There is no outside structure. The faith has turned from outward to inward, the priority of being in touch with one's own experience. The structure or language of that experience is a direct response, a connected response — not a reaction. The language is on a primal level; it is felt rather than deciphered.

The forms and color in my paintings are adjusted. I search for forms that provoke several associations. A referential cubism, like a finger that is pointing in several directions at the same time. All the directions at once being the location of the experience as though one moment possesses many moments, as though one place contains a thousand places — the complexities of one feeling.

Painting for me is a constant search to hold a feeling tangible. The experience "calls" it, the painting "recalls" it. It allows me to hold it in my hand.

Elaine Lustig Cohen

There is obviously a long tradition of abstract art lying behind my work, but I do not regard myself as a disciple of any single artist as much as an inheritor of a sensibility. For me, abstraction is as much present in figurative, nature painting, but I think of it there as enfleshed abstraction. The reality with which I work is not intellectual or conceptual in any received sense, but rather it is the exploration of pictorial tensions of form and space or colored form structuring space. The illusionary event is always on the picture plane, and it is this which encourages the dialogue between the lines of form and the open space.

My involvement with Brunelleschi, the skin of whose architecture has been called drawing on the wall, moved me to an identical research — an inquiry into the color-line dynamics possible upon a flat surface. By interpreting space optically and in chromatic terms I try to create an illusionary structure, much like Brunelleschi's Pazzi Chapel. To determine space and form is reality.

William Conlon

As a painter, I search for order — a way to order my experiences visually. I work within a bound, a flat space — the rectangle. This surface enables me to attempt through the use of geometry and color to plot the elusive structure of order.

Our culture has evolved an empirical order which governs our laws, languages, values and perceptual formats. Our sciences and philosophies help us by explanation and clarification through theories and discovery about visual order.

Yet someplace exists a visual realm. It lies unseen between a lattice of overlapping and transparent structures, which at times seem random and paradoxical. It may appear not to make sense, to be discontinuous, shifting and weaving through the warping void. But through this complex, simultaneous structure, order may reveal itself for a precious moment out of the corner of the mind's eye.

A visual order that does not reinforce or modify existing cognition about the known world pushes the viewer into experiencing a new cognitive schema which can then be used to see the universe, its objects and spaces in a way never thought possible.

That very glimpse of visual order — no matter how elusory — is what my painting strives to record.

Leonard Contino

As a painter I've never thought in what tradition my roots lie, maybe because I've always thought it far more important to do the work. But I do believe that there is a spiritual flow which we are able to draw upon, and, as a painter, I find it a very natural thing to do. In other words, I let the paintings paint themselves. The thing I try to do in each and every painting is to get that spark to happen, and when I finish each painting I want it to have a life of its own and if it takes two dozen or more layers of paint to get that light to happen from within the painting, then that's what it takes.

For some reason, things happen within the painting. As your eyes move across the canvas it is almost impossible to pick out or focus on any one set image. These paintings tend to be simple, yet I can look at them as constantly changing. The one thing I would stress that I try to do in my work is never do a boring painting.

A good painting works no matter what the style — abstract or representational. The one and only objection I have is directed against the photo realism of the seventies. To reproduce exactly is madness. To do what a camera can do, to take the artist out of the painting, is to be left with a lifeless, technically perfect reproduction.

When painting, the technique can vary from painting to painting. One may take one coat thinly applied to get a certain effect, or it may take tape to get a precise straight line. Whatever it takes, that's what will be done. After the lines are drawn that's just the beginning. It can take a hell of a lot of painting; mostly, it's the discipline.

Susan Crile

The seminal ideas of twentieth century painting were mapped out in the first twenty to twenty-five years of the century — Cubism, Constructivism, Dada, Surrealism, not to mention the work of Cézanne and Matisse.

Since then painting has concerned itself with refining and developing aspects of this fertile ground. Even among the innovators, the move has been towards specialization, towards the reduction of image or subject matter in order to isolate and expand upon one or several elements. The value of the individual painting had become gradually less important than the series or the body of work of which it was a part. This was apparent in what and how one remembered; often the artist's image remained clear in the mind's eye, while the individual painting faded away.

During the last ten years the funneling in process has reversed. Painting has begun to fan out — a reaction to the narrowing of decades and particularly to the fast take, streamlined, "it is what you see" of the sixties. Increasingly there is duality, ambiguity, irony and a renewed sense of time as a dimension in painting.

Once again paintings cannot be taken in at a glance. In fact, often they cannot be taken in from a single point of view. They have asserted themselves into the viewer's space, they are psychologically aggressive, whether literally or perceptually. They include more rather than less. These are paintings which cannot be seen if they are not looked at, and cannot be looked at without a certain amount of discomfort: How to hold multiple perceptions within one's vision and consciousness? It is not unlike the process of thinking itself.

Matisse has been the pivotal influence on my work. As often as I have left him, I have returned always to see something unexpected and new. Chardin was important in the beginning when I painted still-life, and Piero della Francesco has punctuated my thought since I was twenty.

My early paintings were representational, my current ones are abstract. In between there have been various degrees of abstract representation and representational abstraction. I see no particular split between the two. Just as a good representational painting cannot be free of an underlying abstract order, neither can an abstract painting be entirely free of associations. I see it more as a question of subject matter — the choice of abstraction versus representation as parallel to the choice, for example, of landscape painting vs. hard edge, geometric painting. The real split is between painting with content as opposed to painting without content. If a painting is successful its meaning or substance is felt through its material, the paint and how it is painted.

Rachelle Epstein

For me the critical issue in painting today is what it has always been, intention and artistry. They are the concerns that I think about when working on a painting, the outcome of which I hope will be beautiful and challenging. I choose a familiar image, that of a repeated pattern. I then proceed to use it to create an abstraction. My concern with materials is only to get the desired effects I want which at the moment are color and surface. There is no distinction between canvas, image and paint.

Robert Feero

The idea of a single most critical issue seems anachronistic, in terms of my understanding of painting today. We live in an extremely complex time, a time where a massive re-evaluation and redefinition of accepted standards is taking place. This inevitably has an effect on present modernist painting.

Many ironclad ideologies are dissolving, such as the boundaries between abstraction and representation. One is free to utilize information from many different disciplines; yet maintain a clear and specific purpose in one's painting.

The overriding issue present in my painting is the need to combine the visual and cerebral processes in their purist form. By fully exploiting the visual medium of color in collaboration with and in contradiction to a highly integrated geometric structure, one is confronted with a painting that is optically powerful and intellectually challenging.

Much of my historical inspiration is derived from

the Constructivists; people such as Kasmir Malevich and El Lissitzky. The Dutch painters Theo Van Doesburg and Piet Mondrian were strong influences on my work, as was Van Gogh through his dynamic use of color. A more contemporary model is Stuart Davis, with his infinite use of shapes and forms that existed in a space that was both 2-dimensional and 3-dimensional combined with an extraordinary sense of color.

In making paintings that deal with a specific geometry of multiple levels, I find it extremely important to maintain clear and articulate shapes.

Webster's Dictionary defines figuration as: 1) the act of giving figure or determinative form.   2) form, shape, outline.   3) act of representation in figure and shapes; emblematical or typical representation. The act of giving determinative form, (form, shape, outline) refers most accurately to my concept of figuration.

Geometry and color, two separate and independent elements when used together both conflict and coincide, contradicting the logic set up by the interrelated geometric system. At other times they reiterate and underline the dominance of the structural form. It is through this synthetic process of utilizing color and geometry that my paintings become energized and animated and move toward their maximum potential.

Hermine Ford

The first paintings I knew were N.Y. School Abstract Expressionist. They were being made as I grew up in the fifties. From these I learned to love paint and the physical handling of it. From there I looked backwards at the great traditions of European painting and forwards at the developing of new and surprising art. For me there is little conflict between these. In fact, the precarious balance between them is exciting and moving. That is taking all that one loves about paintings already known into an unknown painting.

The art that emerged out of and against abstract expressionism had varying effects on me. For a time I made no art at all. Then I drew from nature. At last I began to make paintings of rectangular fields of varying colors and textures lined up in a horizontal row. Though the mark making in the paintings came from the drawings, I wanted to luxuriate in the paint itself, to free it from representation, or any shape other than the given rectangle of the stretcher bars. In this way I *almost* by-passed the necessity for

having to have an "idea" for a painting, and could be absorbed just by putting down strokes of paint. This was a way of getting myself started and slowly figuring out what kind of pictures I wanted to make. It was a way of dealing with my innate desire to make a painterly surface, lack of compelling ideas for subject matter, and certain minimalist work that was attractive to me at the time. The crucial thing to avoid was a "made-up" form for the paint that was not significant for me.

After a while I wanted more from the blankness of each field. I began to allow the brushing to get large enough so that shapes emerged out of the textures and patterns. The critical issue for me now is to make the forms in the painting a response to, or consequence of, the handling of the paint. This is analagous to nature where form is a consequence of growth or change, either gradual or sudden, normal or abnormal. Sometimes the shapes that I arrive at in a painting through a natural procedure of changing the brush strokes have a look of being unnatural, or at least abrupt. This feels very real to me.

I don't think of my work as specifically metaphorical. I do think of it as being about various kinds of rhythms and tensions in me and in the world. Sometimes the paintings do evoke images for me such as grass or water. But they aren't pictures of such things; they are more like a record of all kinds of physical and emotional sensations.

I've heard myself say many times that there's less difference between abstraction and representation than many people think. I don't entirely believe this because there's obviously an enormous difference between a Goya and a Mondrian. But I do believe that all really good art is essentially abstract, no matter to what degree it is also representational.

Sam Gilliam

My work has evolved from the Washington color painters and certain of the abstract expressionists, such as Pollock, Newman and Hofmann. I feel that my earlier work was particularly concerned with the five better-known Washington color painters: Noland, Louis, Downing, Mehring and Davis, and that it was through their work that I learned to look beyond.

As to my interest in metaphor, I am interested in the historical reference to the artist as self and as subject. In this context, the artist becomes not only maker but also mover. His actions, in terms of his work, tend to imprint and possibly change or influence the direction of a particular time. In brief, if there must be a metaphor, I am interested in the inner landscape of things. About technique, I find myself to be much in awe of process.

I see the most critical issue in painting today as one of continual renewal without repetition or imitation.

Ron Gorchov

Beginning with two questions that I am most often asked: The curved support is a very general realization of my ordinary experience in space. So painting continues to be, for me a space, as well as an object. And by using two marks that are more or less congruent, the work of painting is self-refining. That is to say, the relative fluidity of the space around the one mark say on the left can be carried over to the mark on the right and vice versa.

On one hand I am attempting to materialize states of mind that often are no more than fleeting episodes and yet they require more than a sign, a symbol or even an image. On the other hand the episodes I am speaking of are associated with certain settings and therefore unrepeatable, although I am sure they are common enough as types of inner-feeling. Parallel activity to the episodes of mind that I am trying to describe varies; for example, once Malcolm Morley said to me while he was painting a train wreck and I was taking my leave so he could be alone, "It's all transportation, the paint has to move from here to there and I'm just the night-watchman."

Nancy Graves

My recent paintings (1978) exist as a sequence of layers (or spatial levels) which can be read visually and intellectually. They are about scale: scale which is in the mind's eye. The references are to distances: volumes and negative spaces which initially have been interpreted by means of computers. Scale achieved compositionally through overlaid gestures shifts according to where the eye focuses.

For example, a painting might contain dots indicating a bathymetric painting I did in 1971, or a lunar landscape translated from a geological color system (1972), the linear motif of shaped, relational canvases of '75, or the drawing of eye movements "reading" the bust of Nefertiti, (1971). All refer to stylistic departures as well as diverse possibilities of "mapping": or the measurement of space as an abstract visual entity.

Depth of field through layering exists *vis-à-vis* the (a) superposition of "repeat" images from earlier work, (b) changes in scale and in "marks" ranging from fine detail to large brush strokes, and (c) by varied techniques, such as: impasto, encaustic, spray, wash, matte and gloss surfaces in oil paint. An equivalence is set up between the diversity of scale in the referential abstraction and the techniques utilized. The "meaning" of the painting rests on this equivalency.

Pierre Haubensak

The picture itself, the format, the empty surface and its limits, definitely became the actual subject matter of the statement. The new confrontation with the empty picture led to the contemplation of the emptiness in itself, and then again, unhesitatingly, back to the picture as the subject. To perceive this in all its aspects and to make it the support of its own reflection became the guiding line of my work. The window/door image was the result of this concept. On one side, the formal state of the picture — a rectangle or square, and on the other side, the searching for transparency and light, the inner vision. It is only indirectly the visible appearance of the window.

Richard Hennessy

The pursuit of style is a trap, an attempt to justify the arbitrary through repetition. Only the love and pursuit of knowledge yields the highest results. By constantly aiming at the difficult or impossible, the artist acquires technique — the ability to transform his materials. His newly acquired skills reveal poetry inherent in his medium and in himself, and thus provide him with an ever-widening range of expressive capabilities. Sculpture and "good design" have been confused with painting for so long now that the real thing comes as a shock. But then, when have courage, daring, and imagination ever not been required? The art audience of our times is, in the main, frivolous. It asks very little of the artist, even less of art. But it does insist upon one thing — the validation of its petty, suffocating notions of personality. A patron of the past would never have asked an artist to be *himself*, but, if he ever thought about it, to be everybody. Today, the artist doesn't struggle to be himself, but to *not* be himself: to lose himself in his art, in possibility, in the infinite.

Stewart Hitch

My image has become one central, radial, open and shut shape in the plane. The icons of pop symbolized what the images of painting could be. Duchamp's iconoclasm showed artists a way to invent (whatever we think of his paintings) a way to make their own systems for artmaking, outside the linear chronology of art history, or in reaction to it. Pollock's revolt against academic thought led to the realization that painting could incorporate chance and be about its own processes and structure. A new web of meaning was spun over the plane of reason. Clyfford Still reminds me of my Baptist preacher grandfather. Stubbornly, he does *his* work.

My titles are sometimes metaphorical in so far as they may be titles of songs or common objects, things, nicknames or slang. The image is not necessarily metaphorical or symbolic. My painting is not narrative. I am interested in irony and paradox. The image in my work is not new or old, it is the current result of my painting. It may be emblematic or iconic. I try to give each painting its own sense of presence, beyond the merely physical. I prefer this image for its ambivalence. It has individual and personal qualities without being representative. Its perimeter can be altered, its color must be adjusted, my rules will change.

I feel that structure and figuration in painting must relate to the stretcher bars and support of the ground. Accordingly, a central and radial image, necessarily activated by the diagonals of its perimeter creates a power and impact that is inextricably locked to the vertical-horizontal, the X or cross of the traditional rectangle of painting.

My preference for a direct, if not crude approach to the use of materials and technique is consistent with my distaste for the tricks of the trade and the finesse of academic painting. Pigments and oil are blatant, uncultivated facts. The 'avant-garde' seems academic when compared with the freedom still possible in painting. Today, there is no split between abstraction and representation. Now abstraction is as real as representation.

Bill Jensen

To ignore tradition is to ignore the great breadth and weight of the oceans. It is a wishing well that if someone looks into it someone might see more about themselves. It is like a witch doctor that has cured the ills of society and enabled the artist to express human compassion for centuries.

Meredith Johnson

My work is part of a painterly tradition.

Specifically, it has its sources in the work of Monet, Cézanne, Gauguin, Matisse, and to a degree, Manet and Picasso. I am also particularly interested in the painting of Titian, Veronese and Poussin, and in Japanese prints.

What interests me most in these works is the synthesis which these painters achieved between perception and pictorial language. In their works, the "subject" of the painting, its external visual inspiration, is wholly identified with the expressive construction of the painting, and is inseparable from it.

I think that it is probably impossible to draw a clear distinction between "abstraction" and "representation" in painting and that they form a continuous and possibly indivisible spectrum. The syntax of painting is by nature an abstraction. Veronese's pictorial language represents his ideas no less abstractly than Ad Reinhardt's does — the variance is in the degree to which the painter's initial impulse is external, or generally recognizable to others. When the initial pictorial impulse is recognizable in some manner to the viewer, the abstractness of the painter's language is in fact emphasized and thrown into relief by the tension between the viewer's expectations and the painter's lyricism, arbitrariness, and sense of style. It is this focus on the abstract nature of pictorial syntax which is most interesting to me about representational painting. I am interested in metaphor primarily in the reference to the images or formal syntax of other paintings, rather than in the literary or symbolic sense. The poetry of vision exists independently of literature.

I work in oil paint because it is the most responsive and flexible medium I know. It makes possible a variety of facture, a breadth of color range, a fineness of color distinction, an overall luminosity, and a depth and translucency in the darker tones which cannot be achieved easily in other media.

The painters who interest me most are those who have absorbed and synthesized the richest variety of visual impulses and lyrical energy into their work. The literal and self-referential aspect of much recent painting seems almost autistic in contrast, especially since the independence of pictorial means is now accepted without challenge. I think that the most critical issue in painting today is the development of a broader and more convincing value structure with which to evaluate quality in painting, and the development of a wider and more challenging possibility of "subjects" for painting: of formal ends, so to speak, which are more worthy of the available pictorial means.

Lois Lane

When I was in school I wanted very much to do something new. After working on this for awhile, it occurred to me that I was doing something very old. Painting is so ancient. It must be a very powerful form to have stayed with us for so long.

Vered Lieb

Seeing an El Greco painting ("Storm over Toledo,") when I was ten years old got me very excited about painting. Growing up in New York City one gets to see a lot of paintings in museums and galleries. My parents were both artists and took me to the galleries. Picasso and Pollock were big heroes at my house in the way that Michelangelo was a romantic and heroic figure.

The confusion of our culture during the 60's of fine art with graphic art has occasioned a lot of "shallow art"; that is to say, work which is not imbued with didactic qualities. I don't mean didactic in the sense of a purely mental event, but in terms of the manipulation of materials. When artists went back on the work of the Abstract Expressionists, as I believe happened, what was being rejected was a concept perhaps too big to handle. People like Pollock and DeKooning really made a great revolution, like America's first revolution, but in the arts. We have been liberated as painters to paint; to explore the properties of paint for its own sake, without reference to external or literary subject matter. There is, I believe, a moral issue in this attitude, because we must, as painters, be truthful about how we make something happen in our work. This imperative is serious and hard work, and many painters seem to go instead for a certain "look" which stops short of the truth in some way but passes as art. In painting you have to put time and weight into your canvas. Painting in this serious way has to struggle to a level of acceptance, because

though it may contain some decorative qualities, it cannot be essentially so.

I would not want people to look at my paintings and seek a story or literal reference, however, my work does contain indications of my political and psychological states of being. I think that in the long run all artists of a given time and in a given culture, become anonymous. What is left for the historian in the future is totally metaphorical, artifacts which then are traced back to the reality that stimulated their production.

Rather than figuration I am more involved with color intervals; of passages from one color to another or over another. Figuration in my paintings is limited to geometric form. I attempt to imbue these forms with "weightiness", but it is always with the understanding that the paint itself creates this feeling and not the illusion of perspective. Placing figure on ground is rather challenging for me in that it poses certain questions. If the entire surface of the canvas is of equal validity, and as such has to be treated as one surface (in Persian rugs,) how then do you insert a form (or forms) and maintain that kind of surface integrity?

The only issue is quality.

Joanna Mayor

Keeping an open channel while painting is often the most difficult part of the whole process. There is a constant oscillation between the formal elements of painting and the unconscious response - source. The formal elements give structure, peripheral information to the process. The more fluid information must be translated into a recognizable and then a tangible form. For me, art is an alternative form of healing: inspiration heals.

Robert Moskowitz

My work from the 1960's was involved with an architectural type of space that evolved into a symmetrical corner space. I then began putting spontaneous kinds of marks on the surface of the painting—marks that violated the surface and were abstract on the two-dimensional space. I then got involved with the marks and began reading into some of the markings on a metaphorical level. One of the first recognizable images to appear in a painting was a duck. I was attracted to ducks and thought the head of a duck was a very modern shape. The duck is also a vulnerable form and, realizing this, I added two lines—one on the top and one on the bottom of the painting—which I think of as protection lines. By adding an image to the painting, I was trying to focus on a more central form, something that would pull you in to such an extent that it would almost turn back into an abstraction.

The images are just recognizable enough; if you looked at it long enough you would be able to see it. This relates to the kind of abstraction I am involved with. The ambiguity is always there, but I do not want it to be mystical. I will usually title the painting in such a way that it is clear. In all good work there is a kind of ambiguity, and I am trying to get the image just over that line.

The paintings have a pretense about being grand and elegant, but on the other hand I think they are very threatening. I am involved in quality in the work and the kind of finish on it, even though I do not think that is important. I want to do the paintings in a convincing way, try to get as much as I can into them, and make them as dense as possible. There are many images that I have been attracted to for a long time, and I am very obsessed with them. I am involved with a certain kind of image, even though it may not be totally apparent. Most of the images I use have been so stamped on my brain that they are almost abstract.

Elizabeth Murray

I do not see a linear progression in art, nor do I feel that I should be refuting one phase in order to create the next. The most important issue in art today is to continue doing it with integrity. We are living in a critical time, and art is being threatened. Art is an important part of life and to confuse it with fashion, politics or economics can be very dangerous. Painting is an affirmation of life. The "issues" that surround painting have little relevance to my work. Discussions concerning conceptual art vs. minimal art, for example, create a false fog around the act of making art. It is stultifying.

I love looking at painting, and my work has evolved from the whole tradition of painting. As a young painter, Cézanne and Picasso influenced me the most — I learned the most from them.

I never start a painting from a clear, rational plan or from a complete drawing. I work more impulsively. Often, though, the motivation comes from the desire to make a shape or to get a certain

color. The idea is to enact what happens. Although I have been working with shaped canvases lately, that doesn't mean that I won't go back to painting on canvases that are rectangular. There are shapes and figures in my paintings which refer to forms in nature and to the human body. It is a figurative space. But the shapes are not identifiable with a specific thing. They feel like transformations. Since they are organic shapes, associations created by the viewer become inevitable. But the shape painted actually belongs to itself. The act of painting, which is a solitary one, ultimately teaches the artist about the complexity of painting.

Georges Noel

An artist must be very naive and innocent to dare to be "figurative" after Cézanne, Picasso, Matisse and Munch. An artist must also be very naive and innocent to be "abstract" after Mondrian and Malevich.

If an artist is not certain that he is going to add a little "something" to that which has been done, he should give up.

I believe only in art for art's sake. I reject any relationship between art and politics. "Engagé" art is a false idea. (I was in the Resistance in Alsace as a very young man as a soldier, not as an artist.) The artist's combat takes place on the surface on which he works. The artist does not create for the public, nor for the museums, nor for collectors. He is completely marginal in that sense. To begin with, nobody needs art anyway.

The work of art exists only for those who need to look at it, to hear its message and decipher it. No school can be of use to the artist. I owe everything to that which has been done before me. The means I use come naturally now, after a very slow process of maturation made through hesitant moves and failures, alternating with revelation.

I seek less to be understood than to understand. Whatever success I may have had has been a result of misunderstandings and chance. I couldn't recognize it anyhow — which is probably less proof of innocence than of naiveté.

Pete Omlor

In my painting I make the effort to give my thoughts form — evidence of the seen, derived from what I recognize around me and suspended to form the image of my painting. Metaphor interests me as a means to expand the boundaries of my painting.

Today, I think, there are many clever artists, puzzle-makers. Art does not represent to me a problem which needs solving. It is for the spirit, its essence is in spirit and all I experience becomes part of it. Synthesis replaces analysis in an effort to create a broad range of expression, and it is in this attitude I see the most interesting art of the day taking form.

To make art, there must be a distance. My first response to painting came from the reproductions of religious subjects presented to me by the Ursuline sisters during my grammar school education. Then I recall responding favourably to reproductions of Franz Hals during my high school art classes. It wasn't until I was nineteen that I had my first opportunity to view actual works of art — on a visit to the Cleveland Museum. My attention was first drawn to Hans Hofmann and Rauschenberg. On subsequent visits my interests were divided between Ellsworth Kelly and Philip Guston. The contrasts mattered then as the contrast between a laughing cavalier and martyred saint mattered earlier. It is through those contrasts that my painting first took form. The tradition I most connect with proceeds not from a school or style but of an attitude anchored in observation and experience, not theory — a tempered expressionism.

Materials and techniques are like tools — use the ones that best fit the task. At present I work enamel on screen as well as oil on canvas. I'm finding the latter more flexible and compatible. But, it is not through materials that I expect understanding of my painting.

Peter Pinchbeck

The paintings I am making are the result of a need to resolve disparate elements, in particular the dichotomy between thinking and feeling, structure and sensation. The shapes I use, squares and rectangles, function both as colored volumes and as visual signs. The contrast of the painting is determined by variations of value carried into color; the field, which alternates with the shapes in attracting the viewer's eye, is in effect colored space. When a balanced tension is attained between the colors of shape and field, the painting lives a life of its own in accordance with its own laws of proportion and placement of the plastic entities on its surface.

Although originally a painter, I made a series of three dimensional works in the sixties which were influenced by the early Constructivists and their attempts to take the elements of painting into actual space. After a solo show of painted structures in 1971, I felt the need to use color in a more relational way and gain more control over the perceptual space. Painting in a traditional format was the perfect solution for this direction. I am involved in making every part of the painting equally valid, an idea clarified by Matisse in his painting "The Red Studio" and by Pollock in his overall paintings. The idea of the shape both as a subjective and structural element comes from Malevich, and is in turn derived from the Russian icon, of which another Russian artist, Punin, wrote, "For us, the icon is not so much a work of art as a living organism." Painting needs a formal system or vocabulary to move its ideas forward; Cubism, at one time the major force, has become inapplicable because the overlapping of planes disengages shape from field and creates a Renaissance type of space. The more direct figure-ground situation with a shallower space derived from Matisse and Malevich provides a more modern method of advancing painting at this point.

The shapes I use are not metaphors for anything outside the painting. The geometry of shape, size and placement creates an image which has no counterpart in the real world but exists as an autonomous object. The shapes themselves reflect in part the shape of the canvas and its edge and by their frontality help to control the space within the painting. Although the painting is an autonomous object, it is not an object in the minimalist sense because it uses illusionistic space. The fact that this space, the traditional pictorial space of painting, now feels "real" again, for the first time since the American painting of the fifties, augurs well for the development of painting in the coming decade.

Pure or absolute painting utilizes a concept of geometrical form for structure; because it also encompasses sensation it avoids the sterility of art based solely on ideas. To describe this kind of painting as abstract may be a misnomer. It would be more logical to call a painting of a literal object an abstraction because it is an unreal illusion, whereas a suspended plane of color is real; it is not an abstraction of anything, and represents only itself. The unseen aspects of the painting — the axis of the composition, the felt tension between the shapes — are as real as the unseen gravitational force we experience every day or the unseen changes in temperature to which our bodies respond.

William Ridenhour

What we observe is not painting itself but painting exposed to our method of questioning.

Entropy is a measure of disorder. Or is it?

Susan Rothenberg

I don't have a statement about my work. It's getting more psychological and intuitive.

Mark Schlesinger

In life, once change ceases, death is imminent. This is a natural phenomenon that seems applicable to cultural traditions, as well.

Ancient Japan had a tradition where a specific style of painting was passed on from father to son, generation to generation. This clearly defined structure of inheritance precluded adapting the unexpected, inherent in creative discovery. It maintained a predictability by being closed to any questioning or validating of the culturally accepted. This tradition dissolved and no longer exists.

The Western tradition of art allows for and is dependent on change and thus has survived. Yet, the Western artist has often been confronted by various limits that challenge his creativity. To realize this one has only to recall the conflicts inherent in the artist contracts of the Renaissance or the whims of papal patronage. But, in spite of these, and countless others, the Western artist has demanded the right to make artistic choices that display an extraordinary originality.

If one is aware of the enormity of the creative past, one should understand the dynamics of change in art. As a process in the present it is slow and unpredictable, conserving the past while foretelling no hint of the future. Naturally, each artist's survival has to do with his ability to discover his own apparatus for change, the means of which are never clearly offered. Because of these discoveries then, artists can challenge the desires for and articulate the values of the art of the present.

Gary Stephan

The question in my work is always the same. I see my painting in two very different ways. In one sense making my paintings is like building a window. All the decisions about the object are material changes referring to the thing itself. The marking evident on the window and encasement as a result of dowels, planks, wood grain, and glass, maintain a literal, non-metaphorical location. The other way I think about paintings is as the way things are seen to be in three-dimensional space equated with actual material changes on a two-dimensional plane. These two descriptions are in conflict. In the first case, the painting is an object of actual properties (a window), in the second case the painting is a mental construction (a landscape beyond).

How is it to be that the painting can simultaneously be looked at and through? The history of painting is the dialectic between the thing and the view, painting and picture. I best understand this situation in terms of discrete figures and grounds. The painters in history that are the clearest to me are the shape makers, making those works in which the conflict is most acute. Giotto's struggle with illusion redeems the work, limiting the power of illusion to the integrity of the painting as object. Breughel, Cezanne, and Ryder all show a healthy suspicion of perfect pictorial illusion. They are always admitting to the reality of the paint, the canvas, the shapes of things, both as references to pictorial space and as expressive form flat on the painting; that is to say shaped pieces of paint.

Painting is based on these compromises, making judgements on how the object/image is to be realized. There can be no perfect synthesis between painting/picture; the mixed character is irreducible.

Susanna Tanger

My work evolves indirectly from an aesthetic which is rooted in the constructive tradition. There is a kind of integrity implicit in the reductivist insistence on keeping close to what is essential in the process of making art; that the medium should determine the artist's approach. I believe this need to discover the most characteristic properties of the medium is still the most critical issue in painting today. I have a concern for materials, process, color, line and scale. The paintings are material constructions. They are constituted in space, matter and light and are organized according to structural principles.

I am not interested in painting a subject but, instead, want the painting to refer back to itself so that it is the process of perception and of seeing which is important, not of things seen. My art corresponds to my attitude towards nature but I do not deliberately abstract from nature. I present an image which is pure in the sense that it doesn't intend to represent anything other than itself.

There is a definite split between abstraction and representation. It is similar to the difference between ways of writing in ancient times. A pictograph realistically portrayed the object it represented while an ideograph was an abstract sign. The mechanism of visual perception involves a memory which is schematic rather than representational. Mental images are constructs not copies.

I use both configuration and metaphor in my paintings. The configuration consists of a figure on a field. Its shape and placement are related to the dimensions of the initial support which is usually paper or canvas on a wooden stretcher. The figure is placed in such a way as to create a lack of symmetry. I set up a situation where there is some displacement which calls for adjustment. There is a sort of visual argument between figure positioning, color, line and scale. The figure does not represent a form but is rather a visual metaphor for a hypothesis about seeing. It is a device used to provoke interest in perception, focus, memory, and the conjectural nature of knowledge.

Joan Thorne

During my student years I was interested in the abstract expressionist painters such as Rothko, de Kooning, Gorky and Pollock. Later on I became interested in Cubism, Soutine, Baziotes and Paul Feeley, also Milton Avery's landscapes and Georgia O'Keeffe's paintings. It wasn't until my last year of graduate school that I discovered Lee Krasner and Joan Mitchell. Their work has meant a lot to me, as I had no female model to look at before this time. Cézanne, Van Gogh and El Greco have interested me for twelve years now. Van Gogh's conviction and visionary quality intrigues me, his paint quality is tied up with his vision. Rembrandt's painting holds my fascination for the same reason.

The abstract expressionists approached a painting as a complete risk. I have tried to approach it that way, as if every painting I do may be the last one, and take the kind of risks that would entail.

Content is the most critical issue in painting today. I believe this also is tied up with the issue of a personal vision. The problem in the 60's and 70's was one of painters missing meaning from the act of painting. It's just like someone learning the alphabet and not knowing what to write about. Content has been missing from painting for almost two decades. Perhaps this has been a blessing in disguise because people are now starved for meaning in work and will be ready to look at painting in a new way. I believe content in painting has to be part of the way the painter uses the paint, color and structure in the painting. Painting has to get closer to life to have the conviction that has been missing for so many years. Painting needs to become mortal.

I am not interested in metaphor; I am interested in vision. My painting has something to do with visions or images that have spiritual energy (not religious), having to do with the spirit of being alive as opposed to being dead. The visions, images, come into the painting and occupy a space which is always shifting, they are inseparable from the space they occupy. These images are conceived as the painting happens, they are not preconceived. One could say there is a spirit in the image.

I think of my painting as having opposing and contradictory forces. The images — visions are in the process of becoming or dissolving. The outline of the images is more synthetic and the paint around them is more organic, setting up a tension between vision and environment and vision and space. The linear white parts of the painting act like shells that contain or hold part of the painting. They are also an embodiment of time in the painting, by slicing the space so it has different time sequences. They outline the passage of time. The images also deal with time in the sense they frame infinite space or in some cases finite space. They are not solid. I am interested in creating a painting that is actually doing something while you are looking at it, a painting that has a sense of time happening instead of frozen time.

I work with oil paint because it is the most organic paint I can find. Palette knives appeal to me more than brushes because they record the movement of my body and arm immediately, whereas a brush has a life of its own and I am not interested in that. Body movements and markings are extremely important in my painting. I work wet into wet so the paint remains pliable for a long time. This process came about through a need for content and not technique.

Catharine Warren

My painting comes from a tradition of western painting. This is of course natural because I come from a western cultural tradition; but I have also been influenced by an oriental tradition.

I am not excluding modern American painting. This is where I started. Despite all the years of looking at and studying European masters, when I actually started painting seriously in 1967, I was influenced by the established American abstract painters of the preceding twenty years. I knew that my heroes of the Abstract Expressionist School came from a tradition of western painting, but I was only able to think about *my* connection to them. I believe I am breaking that bond and consequently am able to involve myself with more formal or traditional problems of space and composition. One of the most difficult steps, for me, has been the gradual departure from serial painting. I think that aspect alone, even more than a way of painting, had a strong effect on my work.

It is important to realize the various stages that one goes through and to perceive clearly one's connection to the history of painting. In fact the most critical issue in painting is just that connection and the continual rethinking of the ideas to which painters have always addressed themselves. It is not a question of abstract painting as opposed to representational painting because in both of these lie the possibility to deal with the formal problems of painting. "Content", which is both intellectual and emotional, ultimately must be expressed through formal means.

Thornton Willis

In Abstract Expressionism I rediscover certain values that have been paid too little attention in recent times. I am also aware of and influenced by a great deal that has happened subsequent to the 1950's — Pop Art, for instance, and a certain sensibility which might have been manifest through or particular to that movement. However, I am an intuitive artist working through plastic means by choice, and therefore, when I choose my influences I choose primarily those which are brought to life through these means.

The most critical issue in painting today is to reinstate the importance of painting as a means of expression, taking into consideration Pop Art, Minimal Painting, and other movements of the 60's and 70's, and to reinstate color as a powerful and important element. During some of those years there seemed to be a shift away from painting as a viable and challenging means of expression (the "critical issue" then for painters and painting was one of

survival). I kept on painting and will continue to do so inasmuch as no substitute has ever appealed to me nor offered me greater freedom.

In some sense I believe all art to be metaphor. Painting (my paintings) is metaphorical in the most general way; as metaphor for myself, my perceptions, for the creative process in which fact is transformed to symbol, and in turn symbol is used to suggest emotion. However, "metaphor" is a word that seems to imply my being outside of my work which in some sense is impossible. Actually my painting refers to nothing outside itself, except for those most internal feelings and attitudes which I am able to make contact with through whatever transcendent means while the work is in progress.

With my paintings I attempt to be very direct in my approach. I try for an immediacy in relation to the canvas, and to other materials, of which paint is the main one, and it is with this quick beginning that the foundation for the painting is established. After the initial impact upon the canvas, the "building" of the painting becomes slower and more methodical. Decision making on a conscious level is more important at this stage of making the work than in the beginning stages where the subconscious may at times be in control. In the end it is the total image that is important, and an occasional hint at how it happened suffices for us to experience the spiritual.

Edward Youkilis

In my work, I consider the reconciliation of elements from divergent traditions of painting. Certain words have importance for me. These include:

momentum
repetition
ambiguity
velocity
asymmetry
luminosity

Color separations and printing:
Thorner-Sidney Press, Inc.
Buffalo, New York